# ALL I HAVE

# DREAM

## THE
## BOUDLEAUX AND
## FELICE BRYANT
## STORY

*Lee Wilson*

TWO CREEKS PRESS

*Section headlines are titles of Bryant songs.*

ALL I HAVE TO DO IS DREAM:
THE BOUDLEAUX AND FELICE BRYANT STORY
by Lee Wilson

Published by
TWO CREEKS PRESS
P.O. Box 120847
Nashville, Tennessee 37212

TwoCreeksPress@Hughes.net

Cover & interior design: Bruce Gore | Gore Studio, Inc.
Brentwood, Tennessee

ISBN: 978-0-9976507-2-3

*An earlier, limited-distribution version of this book was
published in 2011 by House of Bryant Publications.*

Felice and Boudleaux Bryant,
Nashville's first professional
songwriters

# THE STORY

## OF BOUDLEAUX AND FELICE BRYANT

### is an American story.

**It's the story** of how a small-town Georgia boy married an Italian girl from Milwaukee. It's the story of how a chance meeting saved a young man from alcohol and a girl from a loveless match. It's the story of how talent and hard work took them from rags to riches. It's as compelling a story as a fairy tale. We all like to think that a pure heart, true love, and hard work lead to fame, fortune, and "happily ever after." The Bryants proved that they do.

One of the most remarkable things about the Bryants is that they met at all. In some ways, they were as different as any two people of the same generation could have been. But in a day when family and family history often determined people's lives, Felice and Boudleaux invented themselves.

*Boudleaux held by his mother Louise Parham Bryant in 1920*

# "COUNTRY BOY"

**B**oudleaux was the treasured oldest son of a small-town Georgia lawyer, Daniel Green Bryant, and his wife, Louise Parham Bryant, a talented cook and gardener. Boudleaux was born in Shellman, Georgia, on February 13, 1920; while Boudleaux was still a baby, the young family moved to Athens, Georgia, to allow Daniel to attend the University of Georgia Law School. After Daniel graduated, the family moved to Moultrie, Georgia, where Daniel Bryant practiced his profession at the Colquitt County Courthouse.

Boudleaux was named for a French soldier, Lucien Boudleaux, who saved Daniel's life during World War I. Daniel and Louise Bryant gave all their children unusual names: Diadorius Boudleaux was followed by a sister, Lafontissee; a brother, Neruda Levigne; a second sister, Danise; and a second brother, Jascha Mascagni. The Bryant children deserved distinctive names—they were all good-looking, smart, and talented. Boudleaux was the crown prince of the family. When Boudleaux was just a boy, his father gave him a guided tour of the University of Georgia campus. The trip was designed to inspire Boudleaux, but it also allowed Daniel to boast that his son, at the age of ten, had already been "through" the University of Georgia.

*Boudleaux with his sister LaFontissee in 1922*

Boudleaux's father, a former singing school teacher, played the mandolin, guitar, piano, trombone, and fiddle. Boudleaux's mother played guitar and mandolin and had an excellent voice and some vocal training. The Bryants watched their progeny carefully for signs of musical ability. When they gave Boudleaux a violin for his fifth birthday, they discovered that he could play it "right off the bat" and started Boudleaux studying music. Boudleaux proved to be a prodigy. He was first instructed by his father, whose dream was that Boudleaux would become a concert violinist. When Boudleaux was six, Daniel Bryant persuaded A. E. Goodwin, a retired Boston Symphony cellist who lived in Moultrie, to take on Boudleaux as his only student. Goodwin tutored him through age sixteen. During this period Boudleaux also studied in Albany, Georgia, with a visiting violin master. Boudleaux knew forty to fifty old-time fiddle breakdowns by the time he was ten. He won many of the local and regional fiddling contests he entered, including a Georgia state championship. As he grew as a musician, he also picked up the guitar, bass, and sousaphone.

"My father was an extraordinary man," Boudleaux said. "He was a lawyer, and in my early years, traveling musicians would come through town all the time and get out on the courthouse square and do what we called then 'busking'—they would play and pass the hat. Daddy worked in the courthouse and he would hear these groups. If he heard something he thought was pretty good, my dad would collar these people and bring them home. Mother would feed them, and they would do their various bits for us. I'd listen and absorb. I knew as many hoedowns as I knew anything else when I was a boy. This added a very important dimension to my understanding of music."

For several summers during his childhood, Boudleaux was an important part of his family's traveling band, which consisted of Daniel and Louise Bryant, one of Louise's brothers, Boudleaux, Lafontissee, and Levigne. Daniel Bryant and his brother-in-law built a trailer to pull behind the family car. It held the family's instruments, clothing, and camping equipment; it was outfitted with a chicken coop to carry live chickens to provide eggs and to be killed, dressed, and fried over a campfire on evenings when the Bryants didn't sing and play for their supper. The family earned their expenses by busking wherever they landed along the way. One of the standard events on these trips was an evening fiddle contest at the general store or town square in whatever small town along their route where the family camped for the night. Daniel Bryant would hawk the contest to the locals and Boudleaux, of course, almost invariably won the competition, claiming the contents of the hat that was passed or whatever prize was donated by a storekeeper looking for an event to enliven business. In 1933 the Bryant family band set off for the Chicago Century of Progress Exposition.

*Boudleaux's father Daniel Green Bryant as a young man*

They repeated the enterprise several years later when they traveled to Dallas to the 1936 Texas Centennial Exposition. The traveling band was a source of some discomfort to the Bryant children. They were amazed at their father's abilities as a huckster, self-conscious when he bragged on their abilities and solicited the audience's applause, and embarrassed when their trailer hit a pothole in downtown Chicago and the chickens escaped the coop and had to be chased and recaptured. To Daniel Bryant, each of these trips amounted to an all-expenses-paid family vacation; to Boudleaux, they were an initiation into the life of the traveling musician.

After graduating from Moultrie High School in 1937, Boudleaux went to Atlanta to live with his Aunt Maymee and Aunt Jewel, his father's sisters. He continued studying classical violin in Atlanta at the Leffingwell School of Music and got a WPA job playing violin with the Atlanta Philharmonic Orchestra during the 1937–38 season. He had free room and board from his aunts, which was important because his allowance from home was only a dollar a week and the symphony paid him only a dollar a day. Soon, in addition to performing with the Philharmonic, Boudleaux began playing classical violin in two part-time jobs. He played with the Carl Pathé Concert Orchestra and, on WSB Radio on Sundays, with the Charlie Jarrell Little Symphony. He also collected records of every kind

*Boudleaux with his violin, late 1930s*

of music that appealed to him, including swing, hillbilly, jazz, and everything he could find by Django Reinhardt. Then one day in 1938 while he was browsing in a music store, Boudleaux met Gene "Uncle Ned" Stripling, a bandleader who inquired whether he knew any hoedowns. Boudleaux auditioned on the spot and was hired to fill in for a fiddler who had quit. The first night the young musician played with Stripling, he earned fifteen dollars, more than he was making in a week at his other jobs. Pretty soon, he was hired as a full-time member of the string band, which was called Uncle Ned and His Texas Wranglers. The band traveled in two Packard automobiles to gigs in and around Georgia. Because Boudleaux

*Boudleaux with another violinist in Atlanta in the late 1930s*

realized he could make more money playing hillbilly music than classical music, he commenced a career playing the fiddle and gave up trying to earn a living playing the violin.

Boudleaux played regularly with Uncle Ned and His Texas Wranglers on "Pop Eckler's Radio Jamboree," a show which was comprised of as many as fourteen acts and originated from various Atlanta theatres. "Pop Eckler's Radio Jamboree" was broadcast, in part, over WSB Radio. Uncle Ned and His Texas Wranglers, all of whom wore western outfits including boots, chaps, guns, and ten-gallon hats, were also regulars on WSB's popular "Cross Roads Follies" show. After a few months with the Wranglers, Boudleaux joined a western-swing band led by Hank Penny, the "King of Hillbilly Bebop"; Boudleaux played "hotshot fiddle," which was closer to jazz fiddle than to the simpler style of a country or western fiddler. The band, Hank Penny and His Radio Cowboys, began appearing on WSB's "Cross Roads Follies" in September 1939. From 1938 to 1940 Boudleaux toured with Penny and played on radio stations in Birmingham,

Chattanooga, and Greenville, South Carolina, before the group returned to Atlanta to perform on the famous "WSB Barn Dance" program.

Broadcast from the WSB studios in Atlanta's Biltmore Hotel and similar in style to the "Grand Ole Opry" broadcast over Nashville's WSM Radio, the Saturday-night "WSB Barn Dance" program was very influential in the history and development of what came to be called country music. The program gave exposure to many performers who later became famous, partly through their appearances on the "WSB Barn Dance." The show first aired on November 16, 1940. Boudleaux performed as a fiddler on at least the second broadcast of the "WSB Barn Dance" on November 23, 1940; he played a tune named "Down Yonder." Another Atlanta-based band, the Pine

## BOUDLEAUX ON SONGWRITING AS A CAREER:

**"UNLESS YOU** feel driven to compose and have all the instincts of a riverboat gambler, you should never seek songwriting as a profession. Unless you know in your heart that you're great, feel in your bones that you're lucky, and think in your soul that God just might let you get away with it, pick something more certain than composing, like chasing the white whale or eradicating the common housefly. We didn't have the benefit of such sage advice. Now it's too late to back up. We made it. Sometimes it pays to be ignorant."

Ridge Boys, recorded some of Boudleaux's compositions for RCA Victor in the late 1930s after hearing them played by the Penny band. Boudleaux can be heard playing on several Vocalion recordings the Penny band later made in Memphis while he was working for radio station WMC there; some of the

*Boudleaux in the late 1930s*

songs the group recorded were Boudleaux's compositions, among them "Tobacco State Swing."

After 1939 the road beckoned. Boudleaux left Atlanta and traveled throughout the South and the Midwest working at nightclubs, hotels, and radio stations in Memphis, Washington, Detroit, Chicago, and Milwaukee, among other cities. Between jobs Boudleaux would head to Moultrie, where he could always get a job performing on

*Boudleaux's 43 military classification card*

NOTICE OF CLASSIFICATION   App. not Req.

Diadorius Boudleaux Bryant
(First name)   (Middle name)   (Last name)

Order No. 5-2224 has been classified in Class 4 F

(Until _____, 19___)
(Insert date for Class II-A and II-B only)

by ☐ Local Board.
☐ Board of Appeal (by vote of ___ to ___).
☐ President.

June 2, 19 43
(Date of mailing)   (Member of local board)

The law requires you, subject to heavy penalty for violation, to have this notice, in addition to your Registration Certificate (Form 2), in your personal possession at all times—to surrender it upon request to authorized officials—to exhibit it upon entering the armed forces, to your commanding officer.

DSS Form 57. (Rev. 11-16-42)

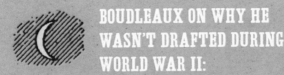

## BOUDLEAUX ON WHY HE WASN'T DRAFTED DURING WORLD WAR II:

"AT THAT TIME I was a heavy drinker. I'd been examined for the draft all over the country—in Atlanta, in Memphis, in Washington, D.C., where I worked for a while, in Detroit, in Chicago. And every time I would go to get examined, I would go in early and I would be so hung over and so absolutely done in that they would turn me down. But the funny thing is that they would turn me down on something different almost every time. One time it was my eyes, one time it was a slipped disk in my back, and another time it was something else. The last time I went in with the grandfather of all hangovers and I couldn't think, I couldn't see straight—I couldn't do anything. This guy just talked to me a little bit and he put down 'severe neurosis' or something.

"But once in Detroit in 1942, I passed. I went down and went through all of the little cubbyholes—they had a cubbyhole for each of the examinations—your heart, your eyes, your this, that, and the other. So they had a little cubbyhole for eye examinations, and I went in and this guy looked at my eyes and said they were O.K. but somehow he forgot to sign that part of the form. I went on around to the end of the line where I was supposed to hand in the form. The guy said, 'Step over there. You are in the Army.' But then he looked at the paper and said, 'Somebody forgot to sign this. Go back through the line.' I went back and there was a different guy there, and he examined me and turned me down."

the town's radio station or in one of its two dance halls. In a pattern that he continued through the early years of his marriage to Felice, Boudleaux would stay with his family and work in Moultrie long enough to build a small stake for going out on the road again. He performed whatever sort of music he could get paid for, including jazz, society, and country. He was a sideman for string bands, for swing groups, for jazz groups. He worked for a short time as a strolling gypsy violinist, a job he considered the most difficult of his career. He played with a country band on WMC Radio in Memphis. At one point in Detroit in 1942 he was hired by the Ford Motor Company as part of a band the corporation maintained to entertain at company events; Boudleaux had to join the old CIO labor union to be carried on the company's payroll as a "mechanic." Sometimes the small bands

## BOUDLEAUX ON WHAT MAKES A SUCCESSFUL SONG:

"I DON'T KNOW what makes a successful song. To carry that further, I would also have to say that nobody else knows. My wife Felice and I have been lucky. For some twenty-two years [he spoke in 1971], we have tossed the musical dice and won. But others, equally talented, have thrown and lost. Why? Again, I don't know. The answer is somewhere beyond our ken, residing in that which is just outside the reach of our normal senses, reposing in a benevolent providence, a bubble of luck, a good karma, or—well, your guess is as good as mine or anybody else's."

he toured with would don western costumes during the east-to-west portion of their tour route and change to tuxedos—and a new name—during their west-to-east return route. And whatever the audience wanted, Boudleaux could play.

By the time he was in his early twenties, the life of a traveling musician was taking its toll

*Felice and her sister Kitty with their dog in the late 1920s*

on Boudleaux. When he was in his late teens he had consulted a doctor about his nervousness on stage. The doctor told him that he could take the edge off his anxiety by taking a swig of whiskey before each performance. Boudleaux followed the doctor's advice only too well. Within a few years, the amiable, intellectual, six-foot-two-inch Georgia fiddler had developed a serious drinking habit, severe enough that it was remarked upon even by his fellow traveling musicians, who were themselves no strangers to hard living. He sometimes hallucinated and called friends to rescue him from whatever dangers he had imagined; he was notorious for the piles of empty liquor bottles that accumulated in the corners of his hotel rooms on the road. Then during an engagement in what hotel promotional literature of the day called the "dazzling and luxurious" cocktail lounge at the

Schroeder Hotel in Milwaukee, he met the girl who would put an end to his binge drinking and give him a direction for his abilities. As a boy Boudleaux had no visions of a fiery, buxom, five-foot-one-and-a-half-inch Italian Catholic midwestern girl like Felice. He did consult an astrologer once, however, in Atlanta, who told him that his was one of the most auspicious charts she had ever seen, that he was going to meet a woman five years younger, and that by their joint efforts they would become wealthy.

## "I'M NOT AFRAID"

**F**elice Bryant was born Matilda Genevieve Scaduto on August 7, 1925 in Milwaukee to Salvatore ("Sam")

*Felice's parents Salvatore Scaduto and Katherine Loverdi Scaduto with Felice's sister Kitty*

Scaduto and Katherine Loverdi Scaduto. Felice was named Matilda, as were all the second daughters in her mother's family. Felice's older sister Kitty had been named Katherine, the designated name for oldest daughters in the Loverdi family. Both Salvatore and Katherine were

Sicilian; Salvatore was of Italian and French heritage, and Katherine was of Italian and Spanish descent.

Salvatore had emigrated to Milwaukee from Palermo, Sicily, sometime in 1912 in the middle of a deluge of Italian immigrants to the U.S. that had begun in the early 1890s and continued unabated through 1914, a year when nearly three hundred thousand Italians left home for a new life in America. In some years of this mass exodus, as many as 90 percent of the emigrating Italians were, like Salvatore, from southern Italy. Salvatore was a dapper, charming, smooth-talking barber. He had wanted to join the Mafia when he reached the U.S., but his Sicilian father wrote to a relative in the U.S. who was a Mafia boss of some influence to ask him not to let Salvatore join the mob. Salvatore, blackballed by his own father, joined the U.S. Army soon after his arrival and served during World War I, thereby earning his citizenship. Later, he contented himself with working as a barber and hanging around the edges of Milwaukee Mafia activities. Family speculation is that because Salvatore was prone to boast, his father had feared he would be killed for talking too much if he were accepted into Mafia circles.

Katherine Loverdi Scaduto had been born in the U.S., in Pennsylvania, of Sicilian immigrant parents. Katherine was a strong-minded woman who tried and failed to fit the box to which her era, culture, and religion sought to confine her. She put up with Salvatore until several years after Felice's birth but divorced him when she could no longer tolerate his habitual philandering. Divorce was

*Downtown Milwaukee in 1930*

such a disgrace and so unheard of that Katherine's own parents made her and her two daughters leave their apartment in the Milwaukee house the Loverdis owned and lived in. Felice would miss this house and daily contact with her Grandmother Matilda Loverdi, despite the fact that her sleep was sometimes disturbed by her Grandfather Carmello Loverdi, who made "the finest [bootleg] Scotch in all Milwaukee." He would regularly wake the young Felice to gain access to the trapdoor under her bed, which led, through a tunnel, to the basement of a house across the street where his liquor was distilled. Katherine ignored her parents' objections to her divorce, freed herself of Salvatore, resumed her maiden name, and used her talents as a cook to create a life for herself as a chef in several Milwaukee restaurants; she was known as "Spaghetti Kate."

**F**elice's childhood was marred by the great bitterness between her parents, both before and after their divorce. Despite family dissension, however, Felice's childhood was relatively happy. She and Kitty biked, skated, and roamed the streets of Milwaukee's Italian enclave; they felt utterly free, but they were watched over by family members and friends as well as the cop on the beat whom their father paid to keep an eye on them. While their mother worked, they often were parked at a movie theatre to watch whatever string of features and shorts was playing that day. Even as a young child, Felice used her lively mind to entertain—she single-handedly re-enacted for neighborhood kids the musicals she saw, taking all the parts and singing all the songs herself, after first assembling the price of her ticket by collecting pennies from the other children.

Felice attended a Catholic elementary school, St. Casimir's, and later, the North Division Milwaukee High School, but she

*Felice's childhood prayer book*

never studied music. Felice's musical education started with her family. She said, "I was singing 'O Sole Mio' when they cut the umbilical cord." Everyone in her large extended family sang and played one or more musical instruments, but no one had any formal musical training—they all sang and played by ear. They often performed at weddings and at other celebrations. "I had pickers all over the family," Felice later said. "Everybody had a mandolin or a guitar and a piano. But I wasn't interested in learning how to play anything. All I wanted to do was sing." She believed that singing Italian folk songs with her family was partly responsible for her later success as a writer of rock and roll and country songs because the feel and themes of the folk songs were universal and were equally applicable to popular American music of her era.

She was also fascinated with words. As a small girl, Felice loved to look at the words written in elegant script

*Felince in the late 1930s*

on letters from Europe that were sent to her family; she would pretend that a letter was a story or a song or an opera and "perform" it for her group of little friends. She said, "I was a showoff. I would give little plays in the backyard. And then when I started kindergarten, if anybody needed anybody to stand up and perform, I stood up. And I

*Felice, her mother, and her sister Kitty, who is dressed as
a bridesmaid for a cousin's wedding*

would sometimes do original works because what I couldn't
memorize I would make up." Noting her daughter's musical
abilities, Felice's mother entered Felice in several Milwaukee
talent contests and allowed her to sing on "Cousin Betty's"
Saturday morning radio show and other kiddie shows on
WEMP Radio and WISN Radio in Milwaukee on and
off from 1930 through 1936. She also performed in live
musicals at the Riverside Theater, the landmark theatre on
Wisconsin Avenue in downtown Milwaukee.

The musical ability Felice inherited from her family
was influenced by the music of the Catholic church. In
addition to the music she heard when she attended mass,

Felice figured out which back doorsteps and which alleys under which windows allowed her to listen to the beautiful devotional compositions sung by nuns in convents and monks in monasteries in the Italian district on the east side of Milwaukee; she regularly stole away to eavesdrop on such otherwise private ecclesiastical services. Her fondness for words and love of music also led her to an early appreciation for poetry; as a young schoolgirl she acquired a copy of *The Best Loved Poems of the American People*, a fat poetry anthology published in 1936, full of poems by many of the Romantics as well as sentimental verses by the likes of Ella Wheeler Wilcox and Edgar A. Guest. She read and reread the poems in the book, absorbing their meter and rhyme and meaning. She began composing her own lyrics to traditional Italian melodies. In a very real way, Felice's early love of music and her favorite poetry book became her introduction to her eventual profession. Through them she gained a familiarity with melody, poetry, rhythm, and popular culture that later informed her own melodies, lyrics, and themes. Like Boudleaux, Felice had real talent from early childhood, but her gifts were not nurtured by her elders, who had no ambition for her other than a secure marriage. She wrote almost obsessively. She said, "My home life was such that if I had anything on my mind, I couldn't spill it to anybody. And so I wrote it."

As a girl Felice didn't know where she was going, but her strong will drew her to the things for which she felt an affinity, and when she met the man who became both her mate and professional partner, she was ready to bloom.

*Felice in Milwaukee just before she met Boudleaux in 1945*

She would later say, "I really wasn't born until I met Boudleaux. All I was before I met Boudleaux was Italian!" In reality she had been preparing for a career as a songwriter her whole life.

## "I DREAMED OF A WEDDING"

**B**oudleaux **was literally** the man of Felice's dreams. When she was only eight, she dreamed of dancing with a tall man with a beard. She could see herself, with long dark hair and wearing a blue chiffon dress, dancing with this man to "their" music. She somehow knew it was *their* music, but she didn't realize at the time what that meant.

She woke her older sister to tell her that she had seen the man she would marry. As Felice grew to young womanhood, however, it must have seemed that her dream was *just* a dream. Katherine Loverdi—by this time remarried to Felice's Greek stepfather George Sokas—made both her daughters quit school after the eighth grade; she pleaded various ill-defined ailments that necessitated that they care for her and assist with the household. Felice worked at a variety of jobs around Milwaukee. She was a movie-theatre usherette, a soda jerk, and, briefly, a roller-derby skater. During World War II, she sang in and directed shows at the USO in Milwaukee.

By the time Felice was in her mid-teens, her mother was in the habit of introducing Felice to wealthy older men whom she hoped her beautiful olive-skinned daughter would marry. Characteristically, Felice bridled at these plans. The only young man she was allowed to go out with unchaperoned was the adolescent Wally Liberace (later known as just "Liberace"), an Italian boy from the neighborhood whom Felice's mother, even then, did not view as a threat to her daughter's reputation. When she was sixteen, Felice married a young sailor she had known since childhood, partly to forestall her mother's further efforts to marry her off to a doctor or businessman and partly because married women seemed to her to have more freedom than unmarried girls. Her family gave her a big church wedding with all the frills and Felice left with her new young husband for the naval base in Texas where he was stationed.

**FELICE ON HER SONGWRITING:**

"**BOUDLEAUX'S** a musician. I am not. I play nothing—I don't play the first thing, not even the doorbell. I don't know any of the rules. I can't read music. I can't pick. I can't quit now, though—I'm a star! God put me here on earth at the same time he put tape machines. That was the way I could create. I hum into a tape recorder. When we write, if it works Boudleaux lets me go. If it's bad, he lets me go and fixes it later. He thinks in terms of melody, music, and everything. I'm lyrics, and so I start with lyrics. But my lyrics have a musical value . . . the words do. And so I compose my melody around my lyrics. But to compose a melody right off the bat, that's not my shtick."

Within two weeks she was back in Milwaukee. She had realized that she loved the young man like a brother rather than like a husband and she was determined not to accept such a bland union, despite the scoldings of her family. Because her new husband was a serviceman stationed in another state, it was possible to put a benign interpretation on the situation: the young wife was living with her family while her husband was in the Navy. But the marriage was over for Felice before she left Texas. She went back to her assortment of service jobs, often working three jobs in order to maintain a wardrobe of stylish clothes. When she wasn't a soda jerk or a theatre usher, she worked as an elevator attendant at Milwaukee's Schroeder Hotel.

# "COME LIVE WITH ME"

**O**n **February 14, 1945,** which was both Valentine's Day and the day after Boudleaux's twenty-fifth birthday, he met the woman the astrologer had foreseen. He was playing violin with a quartet in the cocktail lounge at the Schroeder Hotel in Milwaukee. Since he was temporarily on the wagon, he was headed for the water fountain to get a drink of water. Felice, a shapely and vivacious brown-eyed brunette teenager, was standing beside the elevator she operated at the Schroeder. When Felice saw a tall young man sauntering toward her post at the elevator, she realized that he was literally the man of her dreams. She said, "When I saw Boudleaux, I recognized him! I don't know if you call that love at first sight or 'At last, my friend! I was wondering when you'd come along.' He didn't know who the hell I was, but I somehow knew who he was."

Lacking any better method of engaging him in conversation, she stepped over to the water fountain as he approached and asked him, "Can I buy you a drink?" while she turned the lever that operated the fountain. The fountain malfunctioned, sending a stream of water arcing through the air to hit Boudleaux Bryant squarely on the snowy starched front of the formal shirt he wore with his tuxedo. He forgave Felice for spoiling his stage costume, but he made her pay for the drink—a Coke. Within an hour of their meeting, he introduced her to a friend as his fiancée, and within a few days the two had eloped. They couldn't legally marry at that time because Felice was still married to the young sailor, but they performed their own ceremony privately and knew that they'd never leave each other. "We had a marriage between us," Felice later said. "We didn't go through anybody. Later we legalized it, but at first it was strictly an arrangement between us and God."

Felice's mother was outraged when she found out that her young, married daughter had run away with a traveling musician. She got the FBI to look for the lovers, to no avail. Finally she tracked down Felice and Boudleaux at a Milwaukee hotel. She tried to drag Felice home by her hair when Felice told her she wouldn't leave Boudleaux, breaking Felice's nose in the process. But when Felice's mother finally realized that she could not separate the pair,

*The Schroeder Hotel, Milwaukee, Wisconsin, mid-1940s*

she relented and helped her daughter obtain a divorce. The young lovers couldn't see each other during the months before Felice's divorce was granted, but they secretly stayed in touch—Boudleaux would call Felice at prearranged times on a pay phone at a Walgreen's near where she lived, and he left messages for her in code with friends.

## "SHE WEARS MY RING"

**F**elice and Boudleaux were married officially on September 5, 1945 in Covington, Kentucky, across the

*Boudleaux and Felice in the mid-1940s*

river from Cincinnati, Ohio, where Boudleaux was playing an eight-month engagement at the Gibson Hotel. There was no big wedding for Felice when she said "I do" the second time. They rode around in a cab all day, getting their blood tests and the marriage license, and when they found a minister (who advertised with a neon sign), they drafted the cab driver to serve as their best man. Felice wore a pair of slacks for her second marriage ceremony but Boudleaux wore a tuxedo—his stage clothes—because he had to go to work right after the wedding.

Despite the informality of the marriage ceremony, it was effective. By this time Felice had convinced Boudleaux to grow a goatee so as to resemble more closely the beard-ed man she had dreamed about as a little girl; it was a style that suited the musician, and he wore the goatee off and on throughout the rest of his life. The other change she imposed shortly after the wedding was in Boudleaux's drinking habits—Felice put her little foot down and insisted that he cut back on his regularly excessive drink-ing. Her ultimatum probably saved his life; he never gave up alcohol entirely, but he lived more than four decades longer instead of dying of cirrhosis in his mid-twenties, which he later admitted had been his likely fate. And Boudleaux changed Felice, too. Soon after they met, he rechristened her "Felice"—he felt that neither "Matilda" nor "Tillie" fit her personality. "When Boudleaux and I first met," Felice later said, "I introduced myself as Matilda Scaduto and he said, 'We've got to do something about that "Matilda."' So I said, 'What suits you?'

He said, 'Well, you look jolly, how about "Felice?"' I said, 'Great!' A few days later he said, 'We've got to do something about that "Scaduto."' I said, 'What suits you?' He said, 'Bryant!' I said, 'Great!' Boudleaux titled me." She remained Felice for the rest of her life, even to those who had known her as Tillie in her childhood.

## "OUR HONEYMOON"

**B**oudleaux and Felice had the world before them by the start of 1946, but they weren't yet sure where they were going. Some of the patterns of their early married life were taking shape, however. Felice got bored in Cincinnati. Boudleaux bought her a jar of glycerin and she spent hours blowing bubbles out the window. And she cleaned their small apartment until she couldn't clean any more—"I scrubbed the paint off the walls," she later said. When those activities bored her, she returned to her childhood pastime of writing poetry. When Boudleaux's job in Cincinnati ended, they did what they later always did when they weren't otherwise employed—they headed for Georgia, where Boudleaux had a standing offer to play with Gene Mills and the Twilight Playboys for sixty dollars for a three-night week. They lived in another small apartment at first, then they bought a small house trailer to pull behind their 1937 Oldsmobile; whenever Boudleaux found a paying job outside Moultrie, they traveled in the trailer, and when they retreated to Moultrie between engagements, they lived in it. Boudleaux could be as energetic a promoter as his father in trying to secure paying gigs. Soon after he and Felice married he booked them on a cruise ship as Latin American singers. He figured that he had studied Spanish in high school, that Felice knew a lot of Italian folk songs, that Italian was *nearly* Spanish, and that they could learn a few authentic Latin American songs once they were on board. He argued that once the ship had sailed the cruise passengers were stuck with them—and it *was* three weeks' work—but Felice refused and that was

*Newlyweds Boudleaux and Felice in 1946*

*Boudleaux and Felice in a nightclub in 1945*

the end of their career as Latin American singers. Their families had differing views of the young couple's travels through the South and the Midwest and sometimes farther afield. "We got two different receptions from our families," Felice said. "My family thought we were bums, ramblers. They kept wanting us to settle down. One time they even suggested that if Boudleaux couldn't find any 'steady' work, why didn't he get a job as a bellhop? When we went to Moultrie, the red carpet came out. We were 'world travelers' and were treated like celebrities. And we could leave the babies with Boudleaux's mom at night." There was some cause for Felice's family's concern. Even Boudleaux's better jobs seldom lasted longer than a few months, and he was constantly on the lookout for any way to make a living in music. These were lean days. During one stretch in Chicago, Boudleaux had to wear a layer of newspapers under his jacket to help protect him from the frigid wind because the couple couldn't afford to buy him an overcoat. And once they had to leave a town in the dead of night because they owed money to a grocer there; later, when they were earning more, they returned to pay their debt.

By mid-1946 the Bryants were living temporarily in Oakland, California, where Boudleaux had a job. During this trip Felice found out that she was pregnant with their first child. The couple returned to Milwaukee for the birth; Dane Boudleaux Bryant was born in April 1947 at St. Mary's Hospital, the same Catholic hospital where Felice herself had been born nearly twenty-three years earlier. The baby was to have been named after Daniel Green Bryant but, characteristically, Felice's mother took matters into her own hands and named her new grandson herself. The itinerant couple and their baby crisscrossed the Midwest in their little trailer, with periodic journeys

*Boudleaux with his father and his youngest sister Danise*

south to Georgia, where they parked on Daniel and Louise's small farm, in a field adjoining their backyard.

## "WE COULD"

While Boudleaux worked odd jobs and one-nighters in and around Moultrie, Felice again grew bored. There were only two theatres in Moultrie and their shows changed only once a week. And when Felice decided to learn to shoot pool, her daring caused talk in the town. A woman in a pool hall was a transgression of local custom; the next day there was a sign on the door of the pool hall: "No Women Allowed." "Boudleaux was away so much of the time," Felice later said. "I'd see him just enough

*Boudleaux's musicians' union transfer card from 1944*

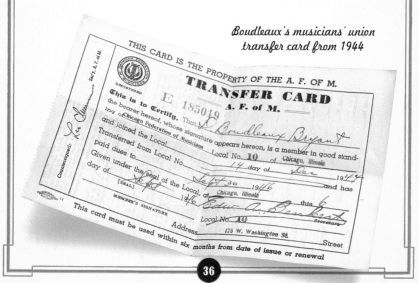

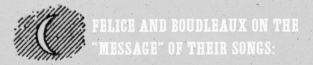

**FELICE AND BOUDLEAUX ON THE "MESSAGE" OF THEIR SONGS:**

**FELICE:** Nothing. Not a darn thing. It's conversation . . . small talk . . . not anything. I'm not a crusader—

**BOUDLEAUX:** We're just trying to write songs that people like, that don't necessarily mean anything. Just songs that people might, in an almost mindless state walking down the street, whistle or hum or sing. We don't have any great message of any sort whatsoever.

**FELICE:** Except love. I mean, that has got to be in there. You know: love is the thing that makes the world go around. Shall I sing the tune?

to say, 'Good morning. Here's your coffee' and 'Better eat. Your supper's getting cold.' We were living in three little rooms and I would clean all day. What do you do when you've got the cleanest house in town? You write songs, that's what! I don't know how we ever managed to have Dane and Del, our two sons, because Boudleaux was never home."

But Felice's boredom and the couple's poverty resulted in a new career for the pair. "We started writing in Moultrie because we had no money. We were married a year before we wrote together. I was cleaning those three rooms—the bedroom, the living room, and this

Boudleaux, standing at center, with one of the bands he played in

Boudleaux, behind the microphone at right of center,
with "Pop Eckler's Radio Jamboree"

Boudleaux, second from right, with Hank Penny's Radio Cowboys

Boudleaux, at right, with the So-Easy Singers

little matchbox of a kitchen. I was getting damn lonely. So I started writing. Boudleaux would come home and ask, 'What did the little woman do today?'—that old jazz. And I'd say, 'Well, I wrote this and I wrote that' and some of it I would sing, because sometimes the words were melodies in themselves." One fateful day in Moultrie, Boudleaux remarked that he thought he could set one of Felice's poems to music. Despite the facts that Boudleaux had written and published a few songs before their marriage and Felice had been writing poetry since she was a girl, neither had known the other was capable of writing a song, and they had never considered collaborating. Felice could compose lyrics and could come up with melodies, but she couldn't write them down. Boudleaux could preserve Felice's melodies on paper as well as compose his own, and he found that her ideas sparked his own creativity. "I couldn't wait until Boudleaux got home," she said later. "He'd get home about one or two in the morning and I'd be wide awake. Bless his heart, we'd get so carried away with this stuff, and he had a six o'clock [a.m.] radio show. So he'd do the radio show and then

*Felice, holding Dane, sitting between her mother and stepfather*

## BOUDLEAUX AND FELICE ON WRITING TOGETHER:

**BOUDLEAUX:** Each of us composes music. Each of us writes lyrics. Each of us writes alone from time to time. There's hardly a day that goes by that we don't get some sort of an idea for a song. A lot of days we get five or six ideas for songs and finish them all. Other days we don't finish anything. Most of the time we write together. She might write a song; she might write a piece of lyric that suggests something to me; or she might have a little tune.

**FELICE:** I will put at least one sentence down, sometimes a paragraph, or maybe just a bridge, but I do have a complete thought and I will write it down.

**BOUDLEAUX:** Felice has more of a compulsion to write than I do. I can go for six months and not write anything more than a note: "I've gone down to the lake and I'm fishing." I do sit around and play my guitar, just thinking. I write constantly in my head and forget it, while she writes constantly and puts it on paper. She has enough lyric material to satisfy—

**FELICE:** A paper shredder for years!

**BOUDLEAUX:** To satisfy twenty collaborators. To some extent I kind of feel it is my obligation to rise to these wonderful ideas she has. My way of working is limited in a sense. I work on what I like or what I think will sound good on a record. If it doesn't fall into that small category, I don't want to get out a piece of paper and write it down. I think I have an ability that enables me to recognize what is good commercially, whether it comes out of her mind or my mind. I think that is one of the qualities that make the difference between a successful songwriter and a not-so-successful songwriter.

*Boudleaux playing fiddle with Gene Mills and the Twilight Playboys, the band with which he performed whenever he was in Moultrie, Georgia*

come back and sleep. It was so much fun working on this stuff together. And since we didn't have any money to go anywhere and we were having so much fun doing this, it was a joy. It really entertained us completely. On Sundays we'd go to his mother's and we'd sing our week's worth of new tunes for the family."

When the couple had accumulated about eighty fin-ished songs, they decided to try to get some of them cut. "We'd go down to the newsstand and get a *Billboard* magazine and just glean every name out of it that seemed to have any address that had anything to do with the music business," Boudleaux later said. "At first, we didn't have any luck whatsoever. But we had a lot of stamps. For over a year, we were sending out about fifteen or twenty letters a day. We'd send a manuscript along with the letter. Ninety-five percent of them came back unopened. Once in a while somebody would write back and say 'We can't use it.'" Nevertheless, they kept at it. As Felice later said, "We had forever. We had more time to push the letters into the mailbox than they had to send them back. The more letters that came back unopened, the more zeroed in Boudleaux became. We had lots of stamps and lots of time. And we didn't know that what we were trying to do was impossible."

In 1948 Boudleaux was hired for a hundred and fifty

*Dane, with Del in a bassinet, in Moultrie in 1949
in front of the Bryants' house trailer*

*Felice helps Del learn to ride a tricycle*

dollars a week by a milling company to promote their product, So-Easy Flour. Boudleaux, bass player Ernie Newton, and two other singers, "Curly" and "Herb," became the "So-Easy Singers." They recorded a group of "transcriptions" in Chicago that was sent out to radio stations all over the country and toured the South promoting So-Easy Flour, staying in each town about two weeks. It was a good job for Boudleaux—good pay and not a lot of work—and, best of all, it gave him some leisure time; at some point during his So-Easy days, he and Felice found time to write their first hit, "Country Boy."

# "I'VE GOT A HOLE IN MY POCKET"

**C**ountry Boy"—and the Bryants—got to Nashville by way of Cincinnati. When Boudleaux was playing a club date in Cincinnati, he looked up his old friend, recording artist Rome Johnson, who was at that time working at WLW Radio there. In one of the first episodes of what would become their standard approach to pitching songs, Felice— who was pregnant with her second son and tending her first, who was a toddler—helped Johnson's wife cook dinner for the group. While the two wives waited for the spaghetti

*Sheet music for the Bryants' first hit song*

COUNTRY BOY
Words and Music By FELICE and BOUDLEAUX BRYANT
Recorded by JIMMY DICKENS for Columbia Records

featured by
Jimmy Dickens

PUBLISHED BY
Milene Music
2510 FRANKLIN ROAD
NASHVILLE 4, TENNESSEE

water to come to a boil, Johnson asked what Boudleaux had been doing. Boudleaux hesitated, but Felice wasn't shy. She stuck her head out of the kitchen and said, "We've been writing songs! Show him 'Country Boy,' Boudleaux."

Johnson liked "Country Boy" and wanted to record it. He called Fred Rose in Nashville to tell him so. Rose was an A&R man for MGM Records and Johnson introduced Boudleaux to him on the phone. Rose wanted a demo, so they made one on Johnson's dining room table with a Wilcox-Gay wire recorder that the singer owned. Rose had other plans for "Country Boy"; he felt that the song would be the perfect follow-up release for Opry star Little Jimmy Dickens's first hit single. Dickens recorded "Country Boy" and his record quickly hit number seven on the *Billboard* chart. Because Opry audiences kept calling Dickens back for encores whenever he performed "Country Boy," Rose asked Felice and Boudleaux to write extra verses; they delivered fourteen additional verses. The cut, and Rose's interest, fueled their ambition and led to their first-ever newspaper interview, with the *Moultrie Observer*, but it didn't do much for their finances—not for a while, anyway. The year finished with a new addition to the Bryant family—in October of 1948, seventeen months after their first son was born, Felice gave birth to a second son, Del René Bryant, in Moultrie, Georgia.

In 1949 Boudleaux got a job playing violin with the band for a tent-show vaudeville-style troupe—Mack and Sandy's Traveling Tent Show. When the troupe folded after only two weeks and left the Bryants stranded in Green Bay,

*Boudleaux and Felice performing for their morning
radio show in Green Bay, Wisconsin on WBAY*

Wisconsin, Boudleaux rented a guitar and a music stand, and
he and Felice gathered their lyric magazines and performed
as a duo act in a local show bar three nights a week, singing
the pop tunes of the day. They also hosted a daytime radio
show on WBAY in Green Bay, "The Coffee Clutch," on
which Felice gave recipes and they performed little skits; the
program made them local celebrities (at seventy-five dollars
a week). But they left Green Bay after a few months for the
simple reason that hosting a radio show was not what they
wanted to do. And winter was coming. They couldn't afford
to live anywhere but their small trailer and because it had
been built in Mississippi, it wasn't a warm enough shelter for
a Wisconsin winter. They headed back to Moultrie, where
Boudleaux could always get work with the Gene Mills band,

**JIMMY DICKENS ON THE BRYANTS:**

"I DID A LOT of Felice and Boudleaux's songs through the years. They're two of the greatest writers who ever lived."

which performed in dance halls in Tifton, Valdosta, and Moultrie and on the radio.

During their trip to Moultrie, their little rolling house escaped the trailer hitch on their car just north of Chicago, rolled backward through a ditch, and came to a halt on the verge of the highway. Miraculously, it wasn't smashed. They had to call a wrecker to extricate it from its resting place between a tree and a telephone pole, however. The cost of the wrecker and of repairing the trailer after the wrecker damaged it in retrieving it from the woods took almost all the money the little family had. They had been making pretty good money in Green Bay, but that had been mostly consumed by payments on their trailer and their car with the too-dim headlights and the cost of hiring a babysitter every night while they worked. When they rolled into Nashville, they had exactly twenty-five cents left. They found a phone booth and used the change to call Fred Rose to ask whether "Country Boy" had earned any money. Fred Rose told them that he had "four hundred and some-odd dollars" in accrued royalties waiting for them. All they had to do was come by to pick up the check. Boudleaux later said, "That four hundred dollars looked like four *million* to us at that time."

After a discouraging start, 1949 proved to be a very good year. During 1949 Boudleaux and Felice scored three more recordings of their songs. Ernie Lee recorded "One Two Three Four Five Foot Six"; the Three Suns, with Rosalie Allen and Elton Britt, recorded "Give Me Some Sugar, Sugar Baby"; and T. Texas Tyler recorded a cover version of "Country Boy." None of the three recordings made the charts, but they offered encouragement to the Bryants, eking out a living for themselves and their boys down in Moultrie.

*A view of downtown Nashville in 1951*

Fred Rose also encouraged them. He asked the Bryants for more material. He sent seventy-five dollars to Boudleaux in Moultrie to pay for train fare and a hotel room, and Boudleaux left for Nashville "with a sack full of songs." Rose took a lot of those songs, but more important, he and Boudleaux became friends. Aware that the Bryants could write more songs than he could use or promote and that they could use the money, Rose asked Nat Tannen, a New York publisher, to come to Nashville the same weekend to meet with Boudleaux; this meeting resulted in a job for Boudleaux as a song plugger for Tannen Music. When he was offered the job, Boudleaux said, "Well, I'll have to have twenty-five dollars a week." Tannen laughed and offered him thirty-five dollars a week. Their musician friends felt that Boudleaux was making a mistake by giving up the steady gigs as a musician that earned him sixty dollars a week in Georgia for a job that would pay him only thirty-five dollars a week, but Boudleaux and Felice knew that the alliance with Nat Tannen was a good one. Felice said, "Everybody thought that we were crazy, but we saw the far vision."

*Fred Rose, the Bryants' publisher and mentor*

Boudleaux negotiated a couple of unusual provisions with Tannen to accommodate the couple's songwriting:

## JIMMY WEBB ON THE BRYANTS:

"WHEN I WAS sixteen years old and in the throes of my first painfully throbbing love affair, I encountered a [then] somewhat obscure Bryant song called 'Love Hurts' on an Everly Brothers album. All of a sudden I realized that a writer's greatest work may not necessarily be his or her most popular work. What would be the definition of the American song without the Bryant tunes? Ask the Beatles. Ask country music's brightest stars. Ask the songwriters who have been deeply influenced, even though some might not realize it."

they didn't have to move to Nashville immediately and Boudleaux was allowed to pitch only songs he and Felice had written. Whatever songs Boudleaux managed to get recorded went to Tannen Music, but the Bryants were also free to write for Fred Rose, so some of their songs went to Acuff-Rose Publishing. Since Boudleaux pitched the Bryant's songs to country artists, this arrangement generally resulted in their country songs going to Tannen. And since Fred Rose had contacts with many of the pop singers of the day, their pop songs usually went to Acuff-Rose. Boudleaux was a pioneer song plugger in Nashville, a town that had not yet become "Music City, U.S.A."

The Bryants' meeting with Fred Rose was fortunate,

both for the young songwriters and for Rose. It was a relationship the Bryants grew to treasure; Felice ultimately called Rose "Pappy." Born in 1897, Rose was a veteran of every aspect of the music industry of the day. He played piano in bars where he worked for tips, wrote several jazz and pop hits, made piano rolls for pay (the other pianist hired to make piano rolls was Fats Waller), broadcast on several Chicago radio stations, and recorded for the Brunswick label. In 1933 he moved to Nashville, where he had a popular show on WSM Radio. He continued to perform on live radio shows and to write songs during his moves to Chicago, New York,

*The 1948 Buick the Bryants bought in Macon, Georgia to finish their journey to Nashville in 1950*

*The Ryman Auditorium in Nashville, home of the Grand Ole Opry*

and Los Angeles. He lived in Hollywood from 1938 to 1942, where he wrote songs for Gene Autry and Roy Rogers movies, among others. In 1942 Rose returned to Nashville and he and Roy Acuff incorporated Acuff-Rose Music, the first major country music publishing house in Nashville. He continued to write songs, several of which became hits, and to act as an unpaid A&R man for MGM Records and other labels. He was instrumental in the careers of the Louvin Brothers, Red Sovine, Bob Wills, and other acts, including, most notably, Hank Williams, for whom he often acted as an expert "song doctor." A devout man who was known for fair dealing, Rose is credited as one of the people who shaped the developing country music industry.

**ONE OF THE GIFTS** the Bryants gave their sons was freedom from racial prejudice, which was endemic in the South—and much of the rest of the U.S.—during their formative years. Both Boudleaux and Felice had encountered prejudice firsthand.

Felice remembered encountering "No Italians Allowed" signs in shop windows when she ventured outside the Italian enclave of her neighborhood. They surprised and hurt the sensitive little girl, who couldn't understand why anyone should object to associating with her. When she was in elementary school, her family lived in Pittsburgh for a couple of years, where her aunt and uncle ran a produce business. Felice was enrolled in a Catholic school, just as she had been in Milwaukee. The difference in Pennsylvania was that it was a Polish—rather than Italian—Catholic school. One of her teachers, a nun, one day called her an "Italian hornhead"—an Italian devil. Angered, the seven-year-old Felice threw an inkwell at the nun. The abuse ceased—Katherine Scaduto saw to that—but the hurt lingered and created in Felice a life-long sympathy for anyone who was less fortunate.

In the early 1960s, during a period when the movement for black civil rights was erupting all over the South, polite black college students in Nashville were badly abused for daring to sit at a downtown Woolworth's lunch counter. Felice, in one of many hardheaded and practical instructions she gave her sons over the years, told them not to get any ideas about being superior because they had white skin. "Everybody stepped on Sicily," she said, meaning, of course, that because of the repeated invasion of Sicily by conquerors of various nations, her sons were the products of centuries of the sort of racial mixing the hysterical Nashville segregationists so feared.

Boudleaux saw a lot of discrimination against African-Americans in south Georgia growing up, but another variety of racial prejudice in Georgia kept from him until he was middle-aged the fact that more than half his ancestors were Cherokee and Creek. Daniel and Louise Bryant had always known that Louise had at least as many Native

American ancestors as those of European descent, but Boudleaux and his siblings grew up believing that all of Daniel Bryant's ancestors hailed from the British Isles. Older Bryant relatives were vague on the topic and several aunts on that side of the family had concocted a grand pedigree for themselves that included European royalty.

Finally, Boudleaux prevailed on one aged uncle, Jesse Israel, to talk. He learned that his Bryant great-grandfather, Daniel's grandfather, had had two mistresses, an African-American woman and a native American woman, in addition to his legal wife, who was white and, as it turned out, childless. Boudleaux was told that the nice white lady in the old photos with Great-Grandfather Bryant was not his great-grandmother, but that he was, instead, the descendant of Great-Grandfather Bryant's Cherokee mistress. Because Jim Crow laws denied any native American in Georgia the right to own land until the 1930s, the Bryant family, despite rather evident characteristic native American facial features, understandably had decided to deny their heritage in order to be able to own their farms and homes. These descendants of the Cherokees who had managed to escape the federal government-ordered forced march of Georgia's peaceable "civilized tribes" along the Trail of Tears to Oklahoma weren't about to let the state take away the property that they had managed to acquire.

Even though Georgia laws were less punitive toward native Americans by the time Boudleaux was a young man, Daniel and Louise Bryant told their children never to mention their native American blood; Boudleaux's parents were afraid that if the racial heritage of the Bryant children were known they wouldn't be allowed to go to college. Boudleaux was amused to learn, late in life, that he was qualified to live on the Indian reservation at Cherokee, North Carolina. He also wrote a handful of Indian songs; typical of these songs is "Thanks a Lot, Columbus," which wryly recounts all the "benefits" Europeans brought to the native Americans.

## "PAY DAY"

In 1950, with some encouragement from Fred Rose, the Bryants moved to Nashville. Nat Tannen had by this time increased Boudleaux's pay to sixty-five dollars a week. The couple loaded their boys in their old car and hitched up their house trailer for the trek from south Georgia to Nashville. Their 1937 Oldsmobile took them and their little trailer as far as Macon, Georgia before it died. Boudleaux found a job there with a dance band—Felice's services as a singer were "thrown in" with no extra pay. They stayed in Macon long enough to earn the money to buy a "new" car—a 1948 Buick—and set out on the second leg of their journey to Tennessee.

### CHET ATKINS ON THE BRYANTS:

"FELICE AND BOUDLEAUX BRYANT were two of the early great songwriters to migrate to Nashville. They showed a lot of people the way. Many of their songs, recorded by the Everly Brothers, greatly influenced the Beatles, who, in turn, influenced the whole world of music. The Bryants changed the direction of music all over the world through their songs for the Everly Brothers."

*Boudleaux and Felice in a mid-1950s publicity portrait
with their names spelled phonetically*

When they arrived in Nashville, they were turned away at one Dickerson Road trailer park because the manager believed that Italian Felice, her part-Cherokee husband, and their two brown-eyed boys were Gypsies. The Bryants finally parked their house trailer at the Rainbow Trailer Court, near the corner of Trinity Lane and Dickerson Road. The Rainbow Trailer Court was a good choice. It was sometimes called "Hillbilly Heaven" because of all the country music performers (Roy Acuff, Eddy Arnold, and Cowboy Copas, among others) who had lived there. And it wasn't far from the Granada Avenue house where another

**PHIL EVERLY ON BOUDLEAUX'S INFLUENCE IN THE LIVES OF THE EVERLY BROTHERS:**

"**WITHOUT** Boudleaux Bryant, we'd be doing some heavy lifting somewhere. I don't care how well you sing, you can't do a damn thing without a song. It's like trying to build a house without a foundation."

VIP-to-be, Chet Atkins, and his wife and daughter would rent an attic apartment when they arrived in Nashville later the same year. Boudleaux Bryant and Chet Atkins didn't know each other yet, but they would become close friends and business associates and would together enhance both of their own careers as well as those of several important recording artists.

The first Saturday night after the family was settled, Boudleaux went to the Grand Ole Opry. He found that he was accepted among the Opry performers as a peer—they had heard him play on WSB. The Bryants became regulars backstage at the Ryman. "We would go to the Grand Ole Opry every Saturday night and Boudleaux would go backstage and jam with the musicians," Felice said. "Because of Boudleaux's musical ability and his work with WSB Radio in Atlanta, we were accepted as a part of the family. When they heard that this picker, this fiddle player, was named Boudleaux Bryant, they remembered him. He was a radio star because of his work with Hank Penny. He played hot country fiddle. Being backstage at the Opry put us in the right place. People would say, 'Hey, Boudleaux, I'm recording next week. Got anything for me?' Boudleaux never said no. Even if we didn't have anything, we would go home and write five or six or seven songs for them to pick from. The invitations for dinner at our house were made backstage. The songs were shown at the house. Or at the trailer, to begin with." Felice and Boudleaux would also claim a table at Tootsie's Orchid Lounge (then called Mom's) across the

## BOUDLEAUX ON THE BRYANTS AND THE EVERLYS:

"WE HAD the opportunity to show the Everlys songs as long as they were here, as long as they were recording. Of course everybody showed them songs. But we did our homework. We wrote a lot of songs oriented toward the Everly Brothers' style. And we were fortunate enough to get something cut every session. And we were even more fortunate in the fact that our songs became big hits.

"I don't think we were that big an influence on them. They were doing what they were doing and we were doing our thing. Our roots lie in country music so we had always had that feeling for close harmony singing. They had also developed that same feel, which is why we started writing for them in the first place. When the Everlys sang, it was like hearing two sweethearts who had been away from their girls too long. That's their forte."

*Boudleaux carrying home fuel and groceries to the Rainbow Trailer Court after a heavy snow in the early 1950s*

*Del as a toddler in front of the Bryants' trailer*

*Boudleaux, Felice, Felice's father Salvatore Scaduto, and Dane*

The young
Bryant family
in the early
1950s

Dane and Del,
pals from the
beginning

Dane and Del
in the
mid-1950s

alley behind the Ryman Auditorium, waiting for Grand Ole Opry artists to drop in for a cold beer between the first and second shows. They had plenty of company at Mom's—it was one of the first stops in town for anyone who wanted to break into music.

The Bryants decided early to concentrate on writing. Their Opry friends couldn't believe that Boudleaux would give up performing for writing and told him "don't put all your eggs in one basket." Fred Rose thought Boudleaux and Felice also had potential as recording artists and in August of 1951 recorded several songs for MGM with them as "Bood and Fileece Bryant"; he himself sang harmony on several of the cuts. They subsequently recorded three more sides for MGM as "Bud and Betty Bryant" but were more interested in writing the songs than singing them. In 1952 songwriter and publisher Frank Loesser, who shared an office with Nat Tannen and who had written the 1950 hit musical *Guys and Dolls*, flew to Nashville to persuade the Bryants to come to New York to write show tunes for him. The Bryants found out about his intentions when they were watching the local news; a news reporter met Loesser at the airport and asked him what brought him to Nashville. "I've come to see Boudleaux and Felice Bryant," he said. Boudleaux and Felice were shocked—and flattered—but they declined to leave Nashville. Writing for Broadway had always been Felice's dream, but the Bryants were building a reputation in Nashville as writers and they had good friends there. Boudleaux told Loesser, "It's home, and we don't

## FELICE ON THE BRYANTS AND THE EVERLYS:

"**THE HARMONY** is something that Boudleaux has always been able to do because of his violin training. He is a freak for harmony. So when the Everlys came along they fell in love with the material that Chet Atkins fell in love with way before the Everlys showed up. Some guy at **WSM** in the staff band—he and his sister did a duet. Rosalie Allen and Elton Britt did duets. We had these beautiful duets long before the Everlys came along, but we needed the Everlys and evidently the Everlys needed us, and we met. And so I don't know who made who, but I tell you, we all had a good time."

want to change our luck." Another reason the Bryants declined Loesser's offer was the advice Fred Rose gave Boudleaux. "Take it from an old [reformed] drunk," Rose told Boudleaux, "you won't last in New York because you have to watch your drinking. The pace there will make you drink too much again. You won't live to be fifty." Felice concurred with him. "I talked to Boudleaux and I said, 'Boudleaux, you know how you are. You know how I am. I'm just a little old housewife. If you decided to disappear from the scene, I couldn't work with those people.' We both thought it would be best for us to stay where we were. And that's what happened."

The Bryants' decision to stay put was a good one; within a few years, they were known all over the world as writers and had become Nashville's first professional songwriters—the first writers in town who made a living as full-time writers, writing songs for other people to record, rather than as writer-performers.

Any song the Bryants wrote that they got cut by a country artist was to be published by Tannen Music, but Nat Tannen allowed Fred Rose first pick for any song he could sell to the pop market. This arrangement allowed Boudleaux and Felice enough elbow room for their versatility—they never had to discard a song because it was "too country" or "too pop." Whatever it was, they could sell it. Their writing and pitching paid off. Between 1950 and

## FELICE ON HOW "WE COULD" WAS WRITTEN:

"WE WERE BROKE. We just didn't have any money to buy presents. Boudleaux had written me a song for my birthday called 'Bless This Day.' So for his birthday I wrote him a song, 'We Could.' After I gave him the song, I said, 'You know, Boudleaux, my song is commercial. I believe it could be recorded and become a hit.' He didn't think so at first, but I proved him wrong. It was recorded and it was a hit every ten years or so. But his song for me was never recorded!"

["We Could" has been recorded by Roy Clark, Jimmy Dickens, George Jones and Tammy Wynette, the Louvin Brothers, Al Martino, George Morgan, the Osborne Brothers, Charley Pride, John Prine, Jim Reeves, and Kitty Wells.]

*Boudleaux in the mid-1950s*

1954, Jimmy Dickens cut six Bryant tunes: "If It Ain't One Thing It's Another," "I'm Little But I'm Loud," "Bessie the Heifer," "It May Be Silly (But Ain't It Fun)," "Waitress, Waitress," and "Out Behind the Barn," which made it to number nine in *Billboard*.

In 1952 Carl Smith recorded his first Bryant composition, "It's a Lovely, Lovely World"; it hit number five in *Billboard*. Smith followed this by cutting "Our Honeymoon," which made it to number six; "Just Wait Till I Get You Alone," which ended at number seven; "Hey, Joe," a number-one hit; and "Back Up, Buddy," which hit number six. "Hey, Joe" was a landmark for the Bryants. It was not only their first number-one country hit, but also it was their first crossover hit. Fred Rose, through his friendship with Mitch Miller, the head of Columbia's pop A&R, gave the song to Frankie Laine. The Bryants helped make Laine's cut a hit; in

*Felice in the mid-1950s*

*Boudleaux and Felice with Wesley Rose in his office at Acuff-Rose*

1953, they left their little boys with Boudleaux's folks in Moultrie and set off on a two-week promotion tour. They drove north up the East Coast on U.S. Highway 1, stopping at every radio station they encountered. "We stopped at any antenna we saw—even a ham antenna!" Felice said later. "And we'd go in and push the record, and it took us two weeks to get up to New York, starting in Savannah. By the time we got to New York, the song was number six on the pop charts." "Hey, Joe" went on to be an international sensation and was cut in several languages. Loretta and Mooney Lynn later credited the Bryants with giving them the idea for their own similar promotion trips; in the early days of Loretta's career

## BOUDLEAUX ON WHAT MAKES A GOOD SONG:

"A **SONG IS** a very simple thing, if you come right down to it. It's an idea that's reduced to just a very few words and not very many notes, and it's got to be something that strikes the ear and is memorable to you, at least for a little while, and something that you want to hear again. That part doesn't change. I don't think that songs differ essentially from what they have been for seventy-five or a hundred years or even longer, maybe. There might be ideas that can be expressed now in language that at one time would not have been permissible. And, of course, the decoration may be a little different—that is, the arrangement may be a little more electronic, may be a little louder, may be a little heavier or more complicated. But as for the basic sound, I don't see that songs have changed that much. And if you show me almost any hit song today, strip away all the window-dressing and leave the bare song, I can probably show you one sixty-five or seventy years old that is essentially the same kind of song, insofar as melodic content and all that is concerned.

"When we're writing a song, we try to write a well-crafted song. If it's supposed to rhyme, it rhymes. If it's supposed to express a thought, it does express the thought and doesn't leave the thing hanging in the air somewhere with loose ends. But after that, we're mainly interested in whether it sounds good. Is the overall impact the kind that we want? And really that sort of thing is not susceptible to analysis. If you really try to analyze a song, you'll analyze it out of existence. You either like the song or you don't. You write it as best you can and then when you've finished with it, if it's appealing and you think it's the sort of thing that would appeal to others, you go with it and try to get it recorded.

"If you ever once have a universal hit, it can become a universal hit all over again—because of the very fact that it still has whatever quality appealed to human nature and made people like it to begin with. Human nature doesn't change very rapidly."

Mooney read everything he could find about the music business and he had read about the Bryants' promotion tour in *Billboard*.

Because they wrote so many Everly Brothers' hits and because those hits are one of the foundations of the rock and roll explosion that began in the mid-1950s, most people don't realize that the Bryants had at least as many big country songs as rock and roll hits. The airwaves— and the record charts—of the early fifties were full of Bryant tunes, both pop and country. "Have a Good Time," the song Felice started (with only a little resentment) when she was stuck in a hot trailer in Georgia with her babies while Boudleaux was on a trip to New York to see Nat Tannen, was recorded by Tony Bennett, again thanks to Fred Rose's connection with Mitch Miller. The Bryants had a string of big country records with Eddy Arnold. Boudleaux's friendship with Chet Atkins (who was working as assistant to Steve Sholes, RCA's head of A&R) ensured them access to Arnold. Eddy Arnold recorded "How's the World Treating You?" (written by Boudleaux and Chet Atkins), "Christmas Can't Be Far Away," "I've Been Thinking," and "The Richest Man (in the World)"; all were hits. And Boudleaux wrote other songs with Chet Atkins, which Atkins recorded,

PUBLISHED BY

Acuff-Rose PUBLICATIONS

2510 FRANKLIN ROAD
NASHVILLE 4, TENNESSEE

MADE IN U.S.A.

in his inimitable style, as instrumentals. The two wrote "Fig Leaf Rag," "Downhill Drag," "Country Gentleman" (which became Atkins's trademark tune), and the bluesy "Midnight," which was recorded by Red Foley. Like the Arnold recordings, the songs Chet Atkins wrote with Boudleaux were hits that became standards. The last song that Hank Williams performed onstage during the last performance of his ill-fated last tour in 1952 was "Midnight."

In 1954 the Bryants left Tannen Music and set up their own publishing company, Showcase Music, with songwriter Vic McAlpin, who was briefly their partner until they bought out his interest in the company. It was a homegrown operation—their offices were in their living room—but they got about forty songs cut within two years, including "Hawkeye," recorded by Frankie Laine and Bobby Lord; "The Richest Man in the World," by Eddy Arnold; and "We Could," by Jimmy Dickens. "We Could" was a song Felice had written for Boudleaux as a birthday present one February when she had no money to buy any more tangible gift; the heartfelt ballad, with its theme of a pair of lovers who can conquer any challenge together, became one of their most recorded songs.

The Bryants had landed in Nashville just when the music business was beginning to *be* a business. And they had a wonderful mentor in Fred Rose, who had an unusual ability to match songs and singers. Once they found Fred Rose and he found them, they couldn't be stopped. As Felice later said, "We survived because we had faith and Fred Rose. We *knew*. And when you *know* you can do it, you don't give up." But in 1954 Fred Rose, a Christian Scientist, ignored signs of a heart attack and died at only fifty-six. The Bryants were devastated. They displayed only a few photos, mostly family photos, in their succession of living rooms, but for many years a framed photo of Fred Rose in his prime occupied a place of honor in their home.

By the end of 1956 Showcase Music was thriving. About this time Wesley Rose, Fred Rose's son, approached the Bryants with the offer of an exclusive publishing agreement. Wesley had worked in Chicago as an accountant for the Standard Oil Company before he came to Nashville in 1945 to manage the business end of his father's publishing company. In December of 1956 Boudleaux and Felice signed an exclusive songwriting contract with Acuff-Rose. In recent years Acuff-Rose had lost its top two writers, Hank Williams and Fred Rose, and needed the Bryants' songs. Showcase Music by then occupied most of the Bryant's living room and all of their time. But they liked Wesley Rose and wanted Fred Rose's company to succeed, so the Bryants agreed to shelve Showcase and to begin writing only for Acuff-Rose. The agreement was the first exclusive publishing agreement the Bryants had ever been offered and one of the first of its sort in Nashville. Before they signed the contract, Boudleaux and Felice negotiated an unusual provision in the contract: if they fulfilled their obligation to write for ten years solely for Acuff-Rose, ownership of their copyrights would come back to them. They had imported this clever bargaining chip from New York, having learned from Frank Loesser of similar provisions in his agreements for his plays. Both Nat Tannen and Fred Rose had refused to agree to an exclusive contract with the Bryants that included such a reversion provision, but Wesley wanted the Bryants and their catalog of Showcase Music songs—including several of their hits—and the Bryants wanted to free themselves from the duties of running a publishing company and to devote all their time to writing.

## "THE RICHEST MAN IN THE WORLD"

It's unlikely that Boudleaux would have become such a successful songwriter without his wife. Even as a young man, he had a philosophical turn of mind and was dreamy rather than practical. Without Felice, most of the melodies he created would have been born in his head and would have died without ever having been written down. Creating music was an amusing and intellectual exercise for Boudleaux, but Felice was driven to write. And because he was so in love with her, Boudleaux became driven, too. Once his ambition had been lit, it burned on its own—both the Bryants worked at their writing every day. Both of them were also very engaged in what could be called their "spaghetti scam."

# "I'D RATHER STAY HOME"

**In an era** when almost the only Italian food available in Nashville came in a can marked "Chef Boy-Ar-Dee," the Bryants used Felice's talents as a cook—and ingredients brought from Milwaukee by relatives—to help pitch their songs. Boudleaux would call home to alert Felice that, in his travels through the Nashville music community, he had netted a producer or a recording artist and that he would be bringing him home for some "real Eye-talian" food. Felice would mobilize her sons, who would tidy the house and help her start dinner, which was veal scaloppine or chicken cacciatore as often as it was spaghetti. While Boudleaux played new songs to the captured producer or artist he had lured home, Felice would be cooking dinner while singing harmony to an occasional lyric and kibitzing with her husband and their guest. By the time the captive had finished the invariably delicious dinner and heard a few more songs, he was usually in a genial mood and almost certainly had been impressed by the songs he had heard.

This method was initiated in the very early days of the Bryants' residence in Nashville, in the small house trailer where they lived for several years after moving to town. Because the trailer was small, the only place a guest could sit to listen to songs was in the combination kitchen and living room area of the trailer. The Bryants would put their young sons to bed in their bedroom in the back of the trailer while they sang and played songs for their dinner guest in the front room. Dane and Del both have fond memories of drifting off to sleep while listening to their parents pitching songs in the other room of the trailer; when the Bryants' guest had left, they would fold out the living room sofa to make a bed, scoop up their sleeping boys, and put them back to bed in the living room.

When they moved from the trailer, the Bryants bought a five-room basement house on Gallatin Road with $6,000 in advances from Fred Rose and Nat Tannen.

*Felice at the breakfast table in the early 1950s in the Bryants' "basement house"*

The basement house lacked the kitchen-living room combination and Felice and Boudleaux missed it, but in 1956, when the couple began to build their dream house on Neptune Drive in a new Hendersonville subdivision on Old Hickory Lake, they made sure that their kitchen and den were combined for easy song pitching.

Pitching their songs at home allowed Felice to contribute to the song pitch while she cooked dinner and, not incidentally, to employ her vivacious personality to charm the visitor. That's how Bob Luman came to cut his biggest hit, the Bryant song "Let's Think About Living." He hadn't liked the song until Felice started singing background parts one night when Luman came to the Bryant home to hear Boudleaux pitch songs. He heard Felice and stopped her: "Wait a minute, Felice. Do that again. I'm beginning to hear this thing." He learned the song that night and went into the studio the next day to record it. It was his only million-selling record.

Felice's cooking produced a lot of cuts, because almost every artist or producer who was based in Nashville or

**FELICE ON WRITING FOR THE EVERLY BROTHERS:**

"THEIR VOICES were so sweet and so innocent that the song had to be void of harshness, of cruelty. It had to have love, tenderness . . . and if anyone was going to be hurt, it would be the singer, because of his naïveté."

## PAUL MCCARTNEY ON THE EVERLY BROTHERS AND THEIR SONGS:

"THE EVERLY BROTHERS were my favorite rock and roll duo in the 1950s. Their harmonies were impeccable and the songs and musicianship in the records excellent. To this day 'All I Have to Do Is Dream' sums up the aching beauty of teenage romance. 'Wake Up, Little Susie' and 'Bye, Bye, Love,' with their acoustic guitar chords, still echo through my mind, as do many of the Everly Brothers' classic hits. They were and still are the very best."

traveled through it during the 1950s and 1960s ate Italian food at least once with the Bryants. At that time Nashville restaurants couldn't serve alcohol; without revenues from liquor, the food suffered. Felice said, "When I first came to Nashville and cooked these dinners, Nashville was a *smaaaall* town with only one restaurant worth going to. Italian cuisine was new to those people. They were not traveled. The country field was quite innocent. That was a little world we were in and we were novel. I fed them until they couldn't move, and Boudleaux would have a captive audience. They had to listen, and to get out, they had to take something. We'd trap 'em!" Boudleaux said, "Felice cooked ten tons of spaghetti."

And pitching songs in person, at home, suited Boudleaux. Sometimes he recorded his own guitar-vocal demos at home with Felice or one of his sons acting as recording engineer or harmony singer; these demos weren't

## BOUDLEAUX AND FELICE ON THE LEDGERS IN WHICH THEY WROTE THEIR SONGS:

**BOUDLEAUX:** We write in these immense, 500-page accounting ledgers.

**FELICE:** When we first came to Nashville Chet Atkins was very nice to us. He used to invite us up to his house. And he'd say, "What have you got, Boudleaux?" And Boudleaux would go through this pocket and then he'd go through that pocket and—

**BOUDLEAUX:** It looked like a comedy routine.

**FELICE:** It really did. And in 1951 Chet said, "Felice, he's got a birthday coming up. Why don't you buy him ledgers like Stephen Foster used to write in?" And I said, "Now that's something I can afford! What kind of ledger?" And he told me what kind. And so I did. We lost a whole raincoat that had eight pockets. And every pocket had a gem in it, we were sure. We lost I don't know how many songs before we started using the ledgers.

**BOUDLEAUX:** Now we're in our fifteenth book [in October 1978].

**FELICE:** With five hundred pages each.

[The Bryants' first ledger is dated February 13, 1951— Boudleaux's 31st birthday. From that birthday, the Bryants wrote every song in one of a succession of ledgers. Felice wrote an endearment to Boudleaux in each new ledger. Boudleaux would write the melody and lyrics for each song the couple composed on a page of one of the big books and would note the successive artists who recorded it and how the recording fared in the charts. At Boudleaux's death, there were sixteen of the ledgers, which are now stored in a large safety-deposit box in a Nashville bank.]

*A few of the many ledgers in which the Bryants wrote their songs*

masterpieces, but they conveyed the songs as Boudleaux thought they should be recorded. But more often, Boudleaux "showed" the Bryant songs himself. Because Boudleaux seldom remembered a song after he wrote it down and because he had lost several that he had thought were hits, early in their career Chet Atkins suggested that the Bryants write their songs in large bound ledgers instead of on the scraps of paper that Boudleaux often misplaced. Boudleaux tried to pitch songs that would fit the artist and if the first few songs didn't work, he'd comb the couple's ledgers for one that did. It was impractical if not impossible to haul the Bryants' ledgers around Nashville, so Boudleaux would pitch their songs at home, armed only with a guitar and his wife's spaghetti.

*Felice's message to Boudleaux in the first of their sixteen song ledgers*

Feb. 13, 1951

To my adorable husband on his 31st birthday:
you're a wonderful father and a very loving husband.
I thank God for you.

Felice

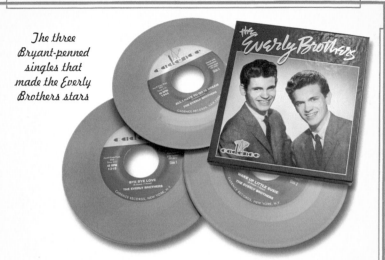

*The three Bryant-penned singles that made the Everly Brothers stars*

The approach worked. Boudleaux had all the songs he and Felice had written right at his fingertips, he was able to talk to the artist personally and to teach him or her the song, and he could suggest arrangements or, as often happened in the case of songs to be recorded within the next few days; he could pick up the phone, call the arranger hired for the album, and sing and play the melody directly to him. Boudleaux also attended as many actual recording sessions as possible, for the same reasons—he could help with the production if necessary. He also knew that it was more likely that the producer or artist would actually record one of the Bryants' songs if he was present.

## "IT'S A LOVELY, LOVELY WORLD"

**T**he Bryants had their greatest success after signing with Acuff-Rose, with the many Everly Brothers hits of the late fifties. It was a good match. The Bryants were parents of two young boys who were as close in age as Don and Phil Everly, and not much younger, so they were sympathetic with the viewpoints of adolescent boys. And the Everlys, with their haunting harmonies, could deliver the Bryants' sweet melodies and naïve lyrics convincingly. The Bryants' songs, delivered by the Everlys, spoke to the burgeoning teen culture, which was just beginning to become fully aware of itself. The Everlys were managed by Wesley Rose, so he was glad to have them record songs by Acuff-Rose writers. This arrangement was both wonderful and, later, unfortunate.

For two years before Felice and Boudleaux met the Everly Brothers, Boudleaux had been hearing from his barber, Ike Everly, that his two sons could sing. Boudleaux told Ike he'd like to hear them some time, but the meeting was never scheduled. And Felice met the brothers when

*Boudleaux and Felice accepting an award at a BMI dinner in New York in the mid-1950s*

she sang on a Nashville TV show, but she was nervous about performing and sang an Irving Berlin tune instead of one of the songs she and Boudleaux had written.

After being turned down by almost everyone in Nashville, the Everlys were signed to a six-month contract with Columbia Records. They cut four country sides that neither they nor the record company liked; only two

*The original manuscript for "Bye, Bye, Love"*

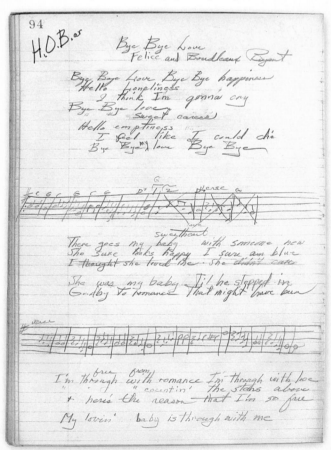

CHET ATKINS ON THE
EVERLY BROTHERS:

"BEFORE THE BEATLES, there were the
Everly Brothers."

of these recordings were released and their contract was
not renewed. Chet Atkins continued to try to help the
brothers during the next two years, standing with them
in the alley behind the Ryman Auditorium on Saturday
nights, introducing them to Opry performers and stars
who crossed the alley on their way to Tootsie's for a beer.
He took them to every record label; all of them turned
down the brothers from Kentucky. Don was twenty and
Phil was eighteen, and they were tired of knocking on
doors in Nashville and tired of being broke. Then Archie
Bleyer came to town looking for a country act. Bleyer had
been the bandleader for the popular Arthur Godfrey television variety show. He signed the brothers to Cadence
Records after Wesley Rose, who met the Everlys through
Chet Atkins, played the Everlys' audition tape for him.
The first songs the Bryants showed the Everlys were some
of the duets they had written for other acts. They felt
that if a song was well written, it could be recorded in
various styles and still work, and that the arrangement of
the song, rather than the melody or lyrics, made it either
country or pop. This is evident in the fact that "Bye,

Bye, Love" was originally written for Johnny and Jack, who were a popular country duet act. That song, written in 1956 in the car as the Bryant family drove to the site in Hendersonville, Tennessee where their new house was being built, was turned down by Johnny and Jack and a lot of other people before it was recorded by the Everlys

*The first pages of the original manuscript for "Wake Up, Little Susie"*

on March 1, 1957. The Everlys, who were ready to call it quits in Nashville and join their father, who was by then working construction in Indiana, were just happy to work for the sixty-four-dollar session fee. The musicians who worked the "Bye, Bye, Love" session stood around talking after the session, saying enthusiastically that the recording was going to be a smash hit. Word got out

207

*The original manuscript for "All I Have to Do Is Dream"*

that something unusual had happened in the studio when the Everly Brothers first recorded a song by Boudleaux and Felice Bryant, and there was a "buzz" along Music Row just days later. The simple but powerful lyrics of the song, the plaintive melody, Don Everly's distinctive guitar playing, and the beautiful Everly close harmonies ensured that the record would not disappear without a trace, as the first Everly records had. In fact, the Everlys' first Cadence record heralded a string of recordings that remain among the finest and most popular Nashville has ever produced.

That year—1957—proved to be an *annus mirabilis* for both the Bryants and the Everlys. Beginning in May of 1957 with the release of "Bye, Bye, Love," the record charts saw a parade of Bryant-written Everly recordings. "Bye, Bye, Love" was the first song of the Bryants that the Everlys recorded and their first hit. Felice said, "Cadence decided to open up in the country field. They had three

## BOUDLEAUX ON THE EVERLY BROTHERS' INFLUENCE:

"**THEY PROBABLY** had more influence than the Beatles because they stamped a style on the whole business that will last for generations. That is not belittling the importance of the Beatles at all, but the Everlys were in at the start when rock music was not widely accepted. They were the bridge to the Beatles, who developed the sound further. The Beatles could not have achieved all they did if the foundations had not previously been laid by Don and Phil, and all the others. The Everlys made the general public, as well as the aspiring artist, aware that harmony was a very merchantable commodity. Quite a few harmony acts came out at that time, and then that eventually spread into large groups which were influenced by having heard the Everly Brothers. I think that they did exercise a tremendous influence on what has become our contemporary pop music."

**BOUDLEAUX:** We were building our house in Hendersonville on Old Hickory Lake. At the time we were living in a basement house on Gallatin Road. While the lake house was going up, I was tremendously excited about it, and so was Felice. I would get up every morning and I'd be on the building site the same time the carpenters showed up, and I'd stay there all day. Well, on the way I'd have a little piece of paper and I'd jot down ideas and titles. On this particular morning the boys were in the back seat of the car, and Felice and I were just trying to get ideas on the way to the house site.

**FELICE:** He said, "I've got the perfect start for a song for Johnny and Jack. I know it's going to be a hit. I've got to stop." So he stops the car before we turn into our new subdivision. I'm dying to hear it, so I said, "O.K., what is it?" He says "Bye, bye, love. Bye, bye, happiness. Hello, emptiness. I think I'm gonna cry." And I thought, Great. Fine. I said, "That's it?" He said, "Well, it isn't finished yet." So we started working on that song then and there and we worked on it at the house site, and when we got home that night, we put together what we had and finished it up. And it was a good song, but he was so up in the air for it. He said, "It's going to be a hit. I just know it. I can feel it in my bones." And I said, "Well, that's nice."

**BOUDLEAUX:** It was turned down by exactly thirty people. I really had a feeling that this song was a hit, and I kept track of everybody I showed it to. It was shown to a lot of people. At that time we were at Acuff-Rose and I showed it to anybody who walked in looking for material. It was turned down by thirty people. I was about to lose my confidence in it. But then I showed it to the Everlys. It was the first thing I showed the Everlys and the first song they ever cut on Cadence. The fates were with us. It was right for the Everlys and the fates made everyone else turn it down.

**FELICE:** The day the Everlys recorded the song, we were all at the studio and Don was doodling on the guitar during a break. And Boudleaux said "What is that?" Don told him it was a Bo Diddley lick. Boudleaux asked him to repeat it. Then he said "Put that on the front of 'Bye, Bye, Love.'" And Boudleaux sat down with him and they went through it and it worked.

**BOUDLEAUX:** They never had a hit until they did "Bye, Bye, Love"—that was their first hit. They had been on Columbia and had done one session which was an absolute total bomb. I don't think that I ever heard those cuts but they were very ashamed of the songs they recorded and wouldn't plug them and wouldn't play them, and as a result the record got lost. I don't know anything about that record except that no one ever heard those songs but them and maybe Don Law [their producer at Columbia]. Anyway, the first successful record that they had was "Bye, Bye, Love," which sold at that time in the neighborhood of two million records. That was our first record with them and we just had a great big long string of hits with them after that.

["Bye, Bye, Love" was recorded at the RCA Victor studio located on Nashville's McGavock Street, as was "Wake Up, Little Susie." By 1958 the Everlys were recording at RCA's new Studio B, at the corner of what was then Hawkins Street.]

country acts—the Everlys, Gordon Terry, and Anita Carter. Their other artists were considered pop. When 'Bye, Bye, Love' was released, a lot of disc jockeys didn't know that Cadence now had a country division. The country radio stations were apprised of the new division of Cadence, but the pop stations hadn't been. So the pop stations began playing it, too. It was a fluke." The "fluke" launched the talented Everlys, who had been struggling in Nashville, but for several weeks they didn't know the difference the record would make in their lives. Just after recording "Bye, Bye, Love," the Everlys went out on the road with Bill Monroe, playing for ninety dollars a week in a month-long tour of a Grand Ole Opry tent show through Mississippi and Louisiana. They heard from Mel Tillis,

*Del and Dane with their mother in front of their house trailer in about 1950*

## CLIFF RICHARD ON THE EVERLY BROTHERS AND THE BRYANTS:

"AS FAR AS I'm concerned the Everly Brothers were a very necessary part of rock and roll. What the Everly Brothers did was to bring a melodic harmonious sound to what was really an aggressive form of music. I can remember hearing 'All I Have to Do Is Dream' and some of the other stuff and thinking that it was a whole new realm to rock and roll; it just broadened it out, and the best exponent of that style of rock and roll, which was the harmony and the thirds, was the Everly Brothers. The influence the Everly Brothers had on me was more of a total influence because they not only brought harmony to that rock feel, they also had that kind of country ballad side to their career, which was so sensational. And Boudleaux and Felice Bryant writing those very melodic ballads—they triggered off my desire to sing that kind of beautiful melody."

who was also playing the tent show, that Webb Pierce had just covered "Bye, Bye, Love"; Tillis, who had had the same experience several times with his records, told the brothers that the cut by the already established Pierce would become so popular that their own recording of the song would go unnoticed by disc jockeys. They were worried until, returning from the road in Bill Monroe's big, old Cadillac limousine, they heard their cut of "Bye, Bye, Love" playing on the car radio just as they drove into Nashville. The announcer said that the record had made it into the top ten on the *Billboard* chart. Eventually, the Everlys' "Bye, Bye, Love" became a worldwide hit. The Everlys' very first cut for Cadence stayed on the charts for six months and, remarkably, made it to the top of *three* charts—ending at number one on the country chart, number two on the pop chart, and number five on the rhythm and blues chart.

The second Bryant song that the Everlys cut also debuted in 1957. "Wake Up, Little Susie" was banned in Boston by adults who imagined that there was something suggestive in the song's narrative of two teenagers who fall asleep at a movie theatre, but the teens who heard it had no reservations about it. The record made it to number one on the country chart, the pop chart, *and* the rhythm and blues chart.

These hits forced the music industry to take notice of the brothers from Kentucky; *Billboard* voted them "Most Promising Country and Western Vocal Group" and *Cashbox* named them "Best New Pop Group" for 1957. The Everlys appeared on "The Ed Sullivan Show" three times during the year, as well as on other television shows. The handsome teenagers with their big Gibson guitars and sweet country-duet harmonies were natural performers, and they convincingly delivered the songs of teen love and heartache that the Bryants wrote. Their success allowed the Everlys, who had been hitchhiking to get around Nashville, to buy a brand-new blue Oldsmobile 98 sedan with a $5,000 advance from Wesley Rose. They drove it to Chicago to visit their parents and told their father he didn't have to work construction anymore. And they no longer stood in the alley behind the

Ryman Auditorium to meet Opry stars—they became members of the Grand Ole Opry themselves.

In 1958, on the strength of their new fame and popularity, the Everly Brothers set out on an eleven-week, seventy-eight-city U.S. bus tour. It was a rock-and-roll roadshow that featured Chuck Berry, Fats Domino, the Crickets, the Drifters, LaVern Baker, Clyde McPhatter, Eddie Cochran, Paul Anka, and Frankie Lymon and the Teenagers backed by a hip black orchestra from New York. During the tour, Chuck Berry showed them Times Square in New York and bought them their first cheesecake at Lindy's. "Bye, Bye, Love" had catapulted the Everlys into another, alternative universe—the world of rock and roll. The lesson wasn't lost on Phil. He later

## PHIL EVERLY ON THE BRYANTS' SONGS:

"LEAVING [our manager] Wesley Rose was not a problem for us, but missing the Bryant songs was a tremendous problem for us. We were writing our own songs but the Bryants wrote at a higher level. What it amounts to is percentages. If you write a hundred songs and you write three hits in that hundred, you're a genius. At Boudleaux and Felice's level, in their hundred, the percentage of songs that were good was much higher. The Bryants' songs were at such a high level of quality, it was an inspiration to a young writer like me. I compare them to Irving Berlin, because his percentage of great songs was very high also."

**FELICE AND DON EVERLY ON THE BRYANTS, THE EVERLYS, AND WESLEY ROSE:**

**FELICE:** That whole combination of Archie Bleyer, the Everlys, and Boudleaux was spectacular. We were hitting three charts. Everything was working. The only thorn in the damn thing was Wesley Rose.

**DON EVERLY:** It was just a great situation for a while. We had the top Nashville session musicians, and we'd come in with the ideas, the arrangements already figured out, and we'd just go in and go to it. I think a lot of people didn't really understand where it was coming from—particularly Wesley, who thought it was like magic.

**FELICE:** Wesley just got greedy. And he would use the Everlys as a stick. Wesley had good business sense in the beginning, but eventually it became very destructive. He even thought that the lead singer, Don, was the whole show. He didn't understand sibling harmony, that symbiotic relationship. He thought that anybody could do what Phil did.

said, "That's what I like about recording. You sing the song and in three minutes your life can change."

The Everlys' third Bryant recording, "All I Have to Do Is Dream," was released later in 1958, as was "Bird Dog." Both recordings of Bryant songs topped the *Billboard* charts. Other Cadence recordings of Bryant songs followed—at that point everyone connected with the Everlys was eager to replicate the surprise successes that had created an immediate worldwide following for the act. Within three years of recording "Bye, Bye, Love" the Everlys had sold more than thirty million records worldwide—most of them recordings of Bryant tunes.

As Boudleaux later said, "After 'Bye, Bye, Love' came out and was an immediate hit, of course we wanted to get some other songs done by the Everlys, and we started writing just a bundle of songs that were suitable for the Everlys and their harmonies. From then on, every time they had a session we would show them songs. Of course, everybody else in town was showing them songs, too—there was a lot of competition. Archie Bleyer, the Everlys, everybody involved wanted them to have the material that was most suitable for them and wanted them to keep on having hits. It just happened that we always had something that was suitable for them. For every tune that they did—for every one of our songs that they did—we probably wrote ten that could just as easily have been done, but of the ten that we'd have to show each time, they did one or two. As a result of that we had a lot of songs that were oriented toward their style. We just happened to be fortunate enough to have songs that they liked and that Archie Bleyer liked." The Bryants were very prolific during this period. "We were turning out a hell of a lot of songs at that time," Boudleaux said. "After our two children were put to bed, Felice and I would write, often sitting up all night. Competition was tough and sometimes we'd come up against a blank wall with our writing, but we kept at it."

In all, the Everlys recorded twenty-eight Bryant tunes;

**BOUDLEAUX:** We persevered with "Wake Up, Little Susie" for many hours. I started writing one night, kept trying to get my ideas down, but it just wouldn't happen. Felice took one listen to what I had so far achieved and came up with the final touches that I couldn't get.

**FELICE:** After "Bye, Bye, Love," the Everlys were looking for a song to record as their second single. Boudleaux was working on this song called "Wake Up, Little Susie." I was upstairs and I heard him working on it. We had just moved into our new house and there was no rug in the living room yet. The acoustics were fantastic in that living room. Boudleaux was sitting there with a guitar and was going for a guitar gimmick, like the one Don had come up with at the front of "Bye, Bye, Love." So he started playing that brisk rhythm and then just came out with "Wake up, little Susie, wake up. . . ." I just burst out of the bedroom and said, "That's great!" But he was headed in the wrong direction because the lyrics were too risqué. He had these two kids doing mature things. I ran downstairs and told him, "Boudleaux, that's not going to work." I told him to put them in a drive-in with a boring movie and have them fall asleep and get home late. Our boys fell asleep at the drive-in all the time, so I knew that was feasible. So that's what he did and it became the Everlys' second hit single. But the Catholic church banned it anyway. They just didn't listen to the lyrics. They must have heard Boudleaux's original lyrics by telepathy!

**BOUDLEAUX:** The Everlys liked the song but, like me, they had problems getting it right when they got in the studio. They worked a whole three-hour session on that one song and had to give up. They just couldn't get it right. We all trooped back to the studio the next day and got it down first take. That's the way it happens sometimes.

["Wake Up, Little Susie" did what it was designed to do—it showcased the Everlys' harmonies, appealed to the growing teen pop market, convinced fans that the Everly Brothers weren't just a one-record act, and became an across-the-charts hit.]

*Boudleaux with Acuff-Rose personnel, left to right, Lester Rose,
Wesley Rose, and Bud Brown outside the Acuff-Rose Studio*

many of the records the Everly Brothers made of Bryant
songs were hits and several sold one, two, or even three
million copies, including "Bye, Bye, Love," "Wake Up,
Little Susie," "All I Have to Do Is Dream," "Bird Dog,"
"Devoted to You," "Problems," "Poor Jenny," "Take a
Message to Mary," "Like Strangers," "Always It's You," and
"Sleepless Nights." The hits recorded in Nashville in the
early days of the Everlys' career made them famous around
the world and garnered them the first million-dollar contract
in recording history—with Warner Brothers—after they
left Cadence Records. In later years they rerecorded and
rereleased many of their hits, including the Bryants' songs, in
"best of" and "hits of" albums. And although their popularity

endured even after their heyday in Nashville, they never had better material than the songs written by the Bryants.

## "PROBLEMS"

**T**hen, in 1962, when the Everlys fired Wesley Rose as their manager, he, as the Bryants' publisher, refused to let them have any more Bryant songs. He had also written himself into the Everlys' new Warner Brothers record contract and had veto power over the songs they could release. They were cut off from any more Bryant songs. Nobody but Wesley Rose liked this arrangement, but people weren't so quick to sue in those days. The Bryants had several years left on their ten-year contract with Acuff-Rose and didn't want to get into an open dispute with Wesley Rose. Relations between the Bryants and Wesley Rose became strained, but the animosity the Bryants felt for Rose fueled their determination, and they endured the unpleasant relationship in order to fulfill their obligations under the agreement and regain their copyrights.

Eventually, all the copyrights in the songs the Bryants had written under the agreement (as well as songs in the Showcase Music catalog) did revert to them—but only the *U.S.* copyrights. At the time the publishing agreement was entered, Wesley Rose told Boudleaux that their songs produced so little foreign money that it wasn't really necessary to include a provision for the reversion of foreign copyrights in their contract. The U.S. copyrights for the songs the Bryants wrote under the ten-year Acuff-

Rose agreement are now published by House of Bryant Publications, the company the Bryants formed in 1967 after the expiration of their agreement with Acuff-Rose, but Acuff-Rose (now part of the Sony Music Group) owns those songs originally published by Tannen Music and by Acuff-Rose before 1956 as well as the foreign copyrights for the songs the Bryants wrote under the exclusive publishing agreement they entered with Wesley Rose.

## "DEVOTED TO YOU"

**T**he **Bryants** were good parents and were always attentive to the needs of their sons. Even when the boys were very young and the family was still living in the little travel trailer that had sheltered them on their way to Nashville, the

*Felice and Boudleaux chatting with his mother outside their "basement house"*

*Boudleaux with his parents and his brothers in the kitchen of the Bryants' lake house*

Bryants didn't let their cramped quarters slow them down. In their earliest days in Nashville, they would work every day in that trailer. On days when there was snow up to the hubcaps and the boys were stuck indoors, Dane and Del would go to the back of the trailer and play quietly when it was time for their mom and dad to write. For their part, Felice and Boudleaux knew how to write over whatever their sons were doing. After a session of writing, Felice and Boudleaux would take the boys out to play.

In 1953, with small advances on royalties from both Acuff-Rose and Tannen Music, the Bryants moved from their small trailer into a five-room "basement house" (a small flat-roofed house consisting only of a basement that rose a

Boudleaux and Felice on the back steps of their house on Old Hickory Lake in Hendersonville

The Bryant family at breakfast in the kitchen of their lake house

The Bryant family in the living room of their lake house

"FROM TIME IMMEMORIAL people have sung, chanted, beat drums, danced, and in various other ways, tried to add zest to a sometimes otherwise humdrum life. Man's natural inclination to amuse himself in his idle hours has led to all kinds of artistic results, not the least of which is country music.

"Much of this music will be the folk music of tomorrow. In common with the folk music of all countries, it originated naturally in the fields and small villages among farmers and other laborers to whom no other entertainment was readily available. It began simply, and simplicity has been a distinguishing characteristic of this music ever since. In fact, country music as we know it was born of a romance between a country boy and a flat-top guitar.

"Country music has jumped its boundaries and is exerting a powerful influence on every other popular music idiom. Conversely, rhythm and blues, pop, and rock and roll have had their impact on country music. The country boy now digs the big beat and there is now room in his ear for a bigger variety of instrumental and vocal sounds, plus other innovations, including a slightly more complicated chord structure."

[From the November 9, 1959 issue of *Music Vendor* magazine, the cover of which featured pictures of Boudleaux and Felice; they were called "The King and Queen of Country Songwriters."]

"I DON'T EXACTLY KNOW what it is myself. I don't feel bad about that because I don't think anybody else does either. In fact, as a clear-cut, culturally confined or definable phenomenon, it just doesn't exist. The word 'country,' as applied to music, is roughly on the same level as the words 'home cooking' on a sign.

"I've heard it said that country songs are more sincere or honest. They do generally speak to subject matters of gut interest, such as love, hate, loneliness, happiness, food, booze, living, dying, and so on—but then, so do most other songs."

[From his remarks to the audience during the Bryants' 1974 session at the 92nd Street YM-YWHA in New York City as a part of that organization's "Lyrics and Lyricists Series."]

few feet out of the ground) on Gallatin Road in the middle of what is now the swarming shopping area of Rivergate in Goodlettsville, Tennessee, just north of Nashville. They still wrote at home in the new house. Boudleaux and Felice often wrote at night, when they could count on several hours without interruption. But they didn't forget their sons. After dinner, the couple would supervise their sons' homework. At bedtime the boys would drift off to sleep to the sounds of their father strumming a guitar and their mother singing little bits of whatever song the two were writing. Or they would hear the song pitches their parents were making after feeding dinner to a visiting recording artist

*Clockwise, Wesley Rose, Roy Orbison, Fred Foster, and Boudleaux in the mid-1960s*

*Boudleaux and Felice in 1961*

who was looking for songs to cut. Boudleaux and Felice would often work late into the night, but when the boys woke they found that their parents had laid out the clothes they were to wear to school that day and had polished their shoes for them. Felice would get up to fix breakfast for the boys and to make sure they caught the school bus. Then Boudleaux and Felice would sleep until their sons came home. And when Felice and Boudleaux built their fine lakefront home on Neptune Drive in Hendersonville, they continued to write at home.

"We had Mom and Dad home all the time," Dane says. "A lot of kids didn't have that. They'd be home with us, or we'd get hauled to sessions with them when

## BOUDLEAUX ON THE UPS AND DOWNS OF THE MUSIC BUSINESS:

"**YOU CAN WALK** up and down Music Row, walk into one publishing office and say, 'How's business? What's happening? What's going on?' They'll say, 'It's terrible. There's a recession and it's bad.' And they'll cite you fifteen economic factors that are contributing to a generally bad situation. Then you can walk into the next office and say, 'How are things?' and they'll say, 'Fantastic! It's the best year we've ever had.'

"So it simply boils down to whether or not you have a hit. If you've got a hit, it's a good time. If you don't have a hit, then things are slow. If you don't have a hit and don't have a catalog, then you could very well be hurting. It's about like it always has been. If you have a good catalog, a lot of songs that continually get played, everything rocks along pretty well and there's no big dip or big peak in your graph, whether you have a hit or not. If you have a hit, that just sort of levels things out for a little dry spell that might be coming along later. If you have a few standards that are out there working for you all the time, then that keeps things pretty much on an even keel.

"But operating a publishing company is purely and simply getting a song recorded now and then and collecting the money, knowing how much you charge for it, knowing how to talk to the people who call up and try to bulldoze you into getting a cheaper rate, which is not unknown in the record business."

they were going out, and we knew that we had to sit there and be quiet during the sessions or if they took us to the Opry with them." "I guess every Opry member babysat us backstage at one time or another." Del says, "They wrote everywhere—in the bedroom, at the breakfast table, in the car. We were two of the luckiest kids in the world. A lot of kids used to close their doors and get under their covers and listen to their little radios real quietly at night. My brother and I would open our door and listen to the songs that the world would hear soon."

The involvement of their sons in the family enterprise continued as the Bryants' reputation as songwriters grew. In the 1950s and early 1960s, almost everyone knew everyone else in the Nashville music community and one of the centers of that community was a suburb of Nashville called Hendersonville, which was, at that time, a very small town that had only one stoplight. "Everybody came through our house in those days," Dane says. "Eddy Arnold would pull up to the dock in his big cabin cruiser. Don Gibson, Faron Young, Chet Atkins, the Everlys, Hawkshaw Hawkins, Cowboy Copas, Jimmy Dickens, Roy Orbison, Jim Reeves, Robert Mitchum, the Crickets, Tex Ritter, Patsy Cline, and Burl Ives all came through the house. Some of them were there a lot. Mom and Dad socialized mostly with performers, rather than songwriters. Dad never played one of his songs for another writer until it had been cut, and he seldom wrote with anyone other than my mother. If they did get together with any songwriters, it was always social, never business."

Other industry insiders were also regulars at the

Boudleaux and Felice in 1967

Felice being kissed by Mitch Miller and Boudleaux

**BOUDLEAUX:** Well, we have a song called "Love Hurts" that was written in the early sixties. Roy Orbison had the first record of it. It was a mild hit. Later on the Everlys did a version of it in an album, but never as a single record, and then a few years later, Jimmy Webb recorded it in an album. In fact, it was the only song in the album that he didn't write himself. And then Cher did it in an album, two or three people did it in albums. Jennifer Warnes did it. And then this group called Nazareth did it. The first that I knew of it was one day when I picked up the *Billboard* magazine, and I was looking in a section called "Hits of the World." And in South Africa, there was a song called "Love Hurts" that was number two in South Africa. I thought, Gee, I wonder if that's our song. And I checked it out, and I found that it was. Well, that song went on and took number one in Europe and got in the top ten in every country. It finally got to England, made a big hit, and eventually came overseas by that same group and was in the charts here about ten months. It never did get to number one; it went to number three, but in the process, it sold millions of records. Well, for three years—for three solid years—that song was in the top ten somewhere in the world. That was a sort of milestone for us.

Some of the other songs that have been very busy are "Bye, Bye, Love" and "Raining in My Heart"—that was first done by Buddy Holly and later on done by quite a few people including Ray Price, who had a number one country hit with it. And Dean Martin did it. Anne Murray did a nice version of that one.

"Wake Up, Little Susie" is one of two songs that Paul Simon and Art Garfunkel did in their albums. The last big album that they had was the *Concert in the Park*. They did a concert in Central Park, and they had over five hundred thousand people there. Well, they did "Wake Up, Little

Susie" in the album. "All I Have to Do Is Dream" has been a hit several times. It was a hit by the Everlys and Bobbie Gentry and Glenn Campbell. And then—you won't believe this—Richard Chamberlain had a hit with it, had a top twenty record with "All I Have to Do Is Dream."

FELICE: And then we have a song called "We Could." Every ten years it comes up and it gets in the top ten.

BOUDLEAUX: The last big hit with it was by Charley Pride. He went to number one with it. And "Devoted to You" was a hit to begin with when it was first cut. It was a million seller, and then a few years ago, James Taylor and Carly Simon did it, and it was a big hit all over again. And one of the biggest hits we ever had actually was a song that was a hit one time and never has been a hit since then, but it made its mark.

FELICE: I can't wait to hear which one it is, myself.

BOUDLEAUX: O.K. It was an instrumental called "Mexico." And it was a big hit in this country, and it went to number one in Germany and was number one for ten weeks and sold well over a million records in West Germany alone. Herb Alpert told me it was responsible for his forming the Tijuana Brass. And Paul McCartney has told us that our songs were very influential on the way that the Beatles wrote. The Everlys had been to England, you know, before the Beatles started calling themselves the Beatles. After the Everlys came back home from the tour they did over there, in a club where they were working, the guys that later called themselves the Beatles started calling themselves the For-everlys. We feel that we have made some mark on pop music as it has come to be, although sometimes I can't be too proud of that.

Bryant house. One of Boudleaux's best friends was Chet Atkins. Besides being a talented performer and musician, Atkins was an influential producer for RCA Records. For a while, Roy Orbison and his family came to the Bryant house almost every day to swim or for cookouts. Fred Foster, the head of Monument Records, and Sonny Osborne, of the Osborne Brothers, were both good friends of Boudleaux. And the Bryants continued to be very friendly with several members of Fred Rose's family. The Bryants were part of the group that mourned for Patsy Cline and the other performers killed in the 1963 plane crash that took her life, and they were among the close friends of Roy Orbison who worried about his

Felice and Boudleaux with two members of the Hendersonville High School marching band

*Boudleaux and Felice in the late 1970s*

health and mental state after his wife was killed in a motor-cycle accident and, later, two of his children died in a fire that consumed his house. Before June Carter agreed to marry him, a distraught Johnny Cash left a handwritten letter to her, asking her to take him back, in the Bryant mailbox one night; after some discussion as to what to do about the letter, Boudleaux called June at her mother's house and read the letter to her over the phone.

Some of their friendships changed music history. One Saturday morning, when Fred Foster and his wife Billie and Roy Orbison and his wife Claudette were lingering with Felice and Boudleaux over coffee in the kitchen of the Bryant house, Fred wondered aloud whether he should grow a beard.

Felice fetched one of her eyebrow pencils and drew a beard on Fred's face to test the idea. When the very pale and very blond Roy wondered whether *he* would look better with dark eyebrows, the women obliged him by coloring his almost-invisible blond eyebrows with the same dark pencil. Then Billie had the idea to dye Roy's pale blond hair black. Roy didn't let the women dye his hair that day, but he did have it dyed later, turning himself into the Roy Orbison the public knows.

And Bob Dylan's *Self Portrait* album owes some of its content to a Nashville party. When Dylan was in town, Johnny Cash had a party at the Cash house and invited both Dylan and Boudleaux. The party was filled with Nashville music people and it soon turned into what must have been one of the most memorable "guitar pulls" ever. When the guitar was passed to Boudleaux, he was a little flustered because he and Felice made it a rule never to play unrecorded songs for anyone. He decided to sing two of their recorded tunes: "Take A Message to Mary" and "Take Me as I Am (or Let Me Go)." When Dylan chose songs for *Self Portrait*, both of these tunes were included.

530 WEST MAIN STREET

HENDERSONVILLE, TENN 37075

BOUDLEAUX BRYANT
FELICE BRYANT

*House of Bryant*

Del says, "As children, we didn't really realize that our folks were any different from anyone else's parents, except that we knew they were home more. I knew they did something different, but I grew up thinking everyone was in the music business. I knew there were firemen, doctors, and lawyers and so forth, but that wasn't who came to our house all the time. It didn't really hit us about what they did until the Everly Brothers started recording their songs. After the Everlys hit, then I knew they were different because the kids at school started asking us if we'd ever met Phil and Don. Of course we had—they were only about ten years older than we were and we had fun with them. So we knew them and it wasn't any big deal to us. But then kids started wanting to come home and meet our parents. That was when I became aware that what they did really had an effect on other people."

During these years Boudleaux fell off the wagon occasionally, but Felice saw to it that his drinking never had a serious effect on his life or the life of the Bryant family. "My father drank some, but we didn't grow up with an alcoholic father," Dane says. "That was due to him and to my mother." Dane remembers one afternoon in 1959 or 1960 when Felice told him and Del to go down the street to play with a neighbor boy for a while. "I have to have an argument with your father," she said. "He's drinking again." Del asked, "But why, Mom? He's so sweet when he's drinking." She answered, "I know, but it's not good for him." The boys disappeared for about an hour. When they returned, they found their father in

**BOUDLEAUX:** Good music is good whether it comes from the hills of Kentucky or the sidewalks of New York. I don't think that our songs have really changed that much since we started. When we first came here we were told not to write anything that had more than three chords in it. In a way, that sounds easier, but in another way, it makes it harder, particularly if you hear things you want to expand on and are not able to do it within the format of what you can peddle. As we went along a little bit we started throwing in a few little extra chords here and there—

**FELICE:** And it caught the artist's ear—

**BOUDLEAUX:** Or a change, or a series or progression that became a little different. Especially after we got the Everlys doing some of our songs. I really started adding a few chords.

**FELICE:** It depends on what the artist was able to do, willing to do, and wanted to do. If he was a big enough artist, the producer had to pacify him.

**BOUDLEAUX:** The Everlys were capable of hearing all kinds of chords.

**FELICE:** Oh, they had such big ears!

**Boudleaux:** And they added a little more expansion in harmony than the traditional country sound had. But, actually, I don't think that songs have really changed that much. The format of country songs has enlarged to the extent that they are doing a lot more chords now than were permissible in 1950. They're a little more complicated, a little more sophisticated, but the basics are still the same.

**FELICE:** What was called pop years ago were the things that Willie Nelson does now [1980]. A lot of our songs that were written some time ago and were pop hits are now being accepted in country music. And, anymore, all that country means is the way you pronounce your words, not necessarily how you present the music.

**BOUDLEAUX:** Everybody now thinks country is fashionable and it's helped Nashville to be known as a country music center, but thirty-five or forty years ago there wasn't any designation "country music." There wasn't any literature of country music. People before the advent of television or very much radio, even, had to entertain themselves, and what came to be developed into "country music" really started out of this amateur front-porch home-style performance. That's all it amounted to at that time. Nobody had written any so-called country songs. Anybody who wrote songs, wrote songs! Jimmie Rodgers even considered himself a blues songwriter. What we were writing was what came naturally to us, and it must have been right because the people accepted it.

**FELICE:** But as to what country music is now, I don't know, except that it's a lot more professional than what it used to be.

**Boudleaux:** The songs can be a little more sophisticated structurally, but going all the way back to those times when songs were very simple, if it was a smash then, it could be a smash now. It can be done with the addition of an acre of extra fiddles and all these embellishments that they put on it, and Kenny Rogers could do it and it would be country or Willie could do it and it would be country and sell to country and pop audiences—to everybody.

I don't see any diminution of Nashville as a center. It has become so identifiable with a particular cultural heritage that it's always going to be here just as an historical thing. People are going to come here from now on. The people here have developed a tremendous amount of know-how and so many great musicians have been attracted to this place. That alone is going to keep people coming here to be recorded. There's so much talent here—new talent, old talent, old know-how, new know-how—all getting thrown into the pot all the time. This will be a great music town for a long, long, long time.

**FELICE:** Nashville is the town that says if you've got the talent, come on, we'll listen to you. Nashville is like a big old fat mama. She just says, "You sing, honey? Let mama hear ya!"

the kitchen, eating with a fork from a newly opened jar of figs. Boudleaux was back on the wagon and consoling himself with some of his mother's homemade preserves.

By the time Dane and Del were in their mid-teens, they were important parts of their parents' business activities. Just as Boudleaux and Felice managed to take good care of their boys while working at their craft, their sons learned early to accommodate their parents' writing. As a young boy, Dane learned to operate the board in the small home recording studio in the lake house, and Del sang back-up on demos from an early age. Both stuffed envelopes for promotional mailings of their parents' songs and both helped pitch songs. "We started pitching songs as soon as we were old enough to shut up and pay attention to what was going on around us," Dane says. Having watched their parents pitch and promote their songs since early childhood, in the early 1960s Dane and Del embarked on road trips to promote Bryant songs to radio stations. They had a credit card, their parents' car, and *one* nice leather briefcase big enough to hold twelve-inch record albums—it was embossed with the initials for both boys: "DBB" *and* "DRB." Both Bryant sons continued to work for House of Bryant during and after college. Although House of Bryant was located in a succession of offices away from the Bryant home, it was always definitely a *family* business; in 1971 a secretary for House of Bryant joked that she was the only secretary in the country who worked for a family and three pets—a dog named Taffy, a bird named Tiger, and a squirrel named Clarence. In the early 1970s, when

## SONNY OSBORNE ON WHAT "ROCKY TOP" DID FOR HIS CAREER:

"BOUDLEAUX BRYANT, who wrote 'Rocky Top' [with Felice], 'Georgia Piney Woods,' and 'Muddy Bottom,' called me one night. He said that we had a hit. I said, 'What?' He said, 'Rocky Top.'

"'Rocky Top' had been out three weeks and had sold 84,000 records. That's unheard-of for bluegrass and it's really pretty good for anybody. 'Rocky Top' has since been recorded over a hundred times. It's one of the best-known standard songs in the world. It's equally recognized in Japan and Sweden and Germany—anywhere.

"It really gives me a sense of pleasure to know that they all use our arrangement, that we did that. It opened a door for us that would not have been opened and that has not been opened for any other bluegrass group, except maybe Lester Flatt and Earl Scruggs. It opened the door that has allowed us to go places that no one in our whole side of the business—bluegrass—has been before or since."

they reached their early twenties and became young adults, both Dane and Del left the family nest. Dane left to start his own recording studio and music publishing company and Del went to work for BMI.

## "ROCKY TOP"

**F**rom the late 1950s, the Bryants often retreated to the Tennessee mountain resort town of Gatlinburg to

*Boudleaux and Felice with two of Del's children, Heather and Tremayne*

*Felice and Boudleaux in the mid-1970s—note the photo of Fred Rose over the hearth*

*Felice, Boudleaux, and Dane at a Chet Atkins Day event in 1971*

Boudleaux, Felice, Dane, Del, and other notables at a BMI awards dinner in 1970

Boudleaux and Felice performing on "Hee Haw" with Roy Clark

Felice and Minnie Pearl clowning during a 1970s golf tournament

rest and to write. In the early years, they took their sons, who loved to ride horseback through the mountains. Later, when their sons were older, Boudleaux and Felice went alone. They always stayed at the Gatlinburg Inn, even when it was closed during the winter, and seldom left their room except for meals or to walk, often staying for a month at a time and coming home with fifty or sixty new songs. In the winter, with no other guests at the hotel, they had absolute

*Felice and Boudleaux at the Tennessee legislature when "Rocky Top" was honored as a state song*

*On the field at Neyland Stadium in Knoxville during a 1978 University of Tennessee halftime tribute to the Bryants as writers of "Rocky Top"*

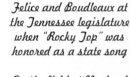

*Boudleaux and Felice laughing it up with Dane and Del at a BMI awards dinner in the mid-1970s*

*Phil Everly, Frances Preston, Felice, and Boudleaux at a 1976 BMI awards dinner*

peace and quiet and could work without distractions.

The mountains inspired them. In fact, Gatlinburg was the birthplace of one of their most famous songs, "Rocky Top." "Rocky Top" has been cut by numerous artists since it was written in 1967, has become the fight song for the University of Tennessee, and was voted a state song by the Tennessee legislature in 1982.

In the late 1970s, the Bryants bought a large old house on the edge of the Great Smoky Mountains National Park

"'ROCKY TOP' was written in room 388 at the Gatlinburg Inn in Gatlinburg, Tennessee. I'll never forget it. It was 1967 and we had been working on an album for Archie Campbell for three whole weeks. It was called *The Golden Years* and we were having a hard time finding positive things to write about growing old. We were on this old stuff, like 'the kids are gone, we're sittin' here rockin' on the front porch, and the dog will soon be dead. Next, you and me, Pa.' I was getting depressed, so I told Boudleaux I wanted to write something happy. I needed something peppy and upbeat and a lot more positive. He said, 'We'll take a break when we get finished.' I said, 'I'm turning gray and getting arthritic.' I refused to keep working and it made him mad. He said, 'You want to write something else? Well, what do you want to write?' I said, 'How about a mountain song, a bluegrass thing, something lively and up-tempo and happy?' Then he banged out a couple of fast lines on his guitar and started singing 'Wish that I was on old Rocky Top, down in the Tennessee hills . . . .' He said, 'How's that?' I said, 'That's fine.' He said, 'We'll call it "Rocky Top."' So we started working on that thing and he had two lines, and I threw in two lines and then he had another line and before you know it was finished. Boudleaux said, 'Good. Now we can get back to work.'

"'Rocky Top' just showed itself up. Boudleaux accepted every line I said, just to get it over with. We got it down on paper in ten minutes and then went back to work on the other project. When we got home, Sonny Osborne had a session coming up on Decca [Records] and called to see if we had anything for them. Boudleaux never said no. Then, after he had hung up, he said to me, 'Do we have anything for the Osbornes?' I said, 'How about that little bluegrass thing we did in Gatlinburg? The one that almost caused us to get a divorce?' I couldn't even remember the title. I hunted up the manuscript—it was still packed with our stuff from the trip. When Sonny came, Boudleaux started to sing. All he had sung was 'Wish that I was on old Rocky Top' when Sonny jumped up and said, 'I'll take it.' I said, 'Sonny, don't you

want to hear the rest of it?' He said, 'That's enough. I want that one.'
And he ran with it."

[The Osbornes had a hit with "Rocky Top" in 1967; it became their sig-
nature song shortly after they first recorded it. Numerous other artists
have since recorded the song, both in the U.S. and around the world.
"Rocky Top" is perhaps the most famous song in bluegrass history. It has
also become an indispensable feature of every University of Tennessee
football game since it was first played by the Pride of the Southland Band
at the UT-Alabama game on October 21, 1972. In 1982 "Rocky Top" was
made an official Tennessee state song by the state legislature; as part
of the ceremonies the Osborne Brothers played and sang "Rocky Top"
on the floor of the General Assembly. In 2002 it was played eighty-eight
times during a six-overtime UT-Arkansas game.]

*The original manuscript for "Rocky Top"*

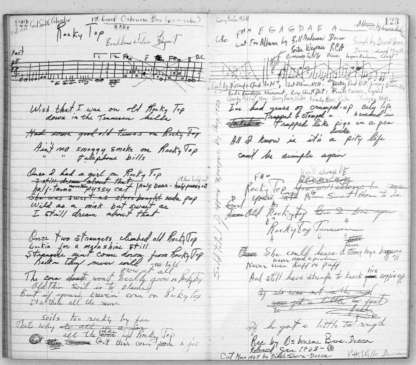

and hired a family of mountain artisans to remodel it. The Bryants moved into their mountain retreat in 1980. They kept working. They wrote several musical plays during their years in Gatlinburg, and, when Boudleaux died, had plans to take at least one of them to Broadway.

## "WE COULD"

**T**he Bryants were well equipped to do what they did—create and influence works of American popular music that helped define country music and early rock

*Felice and Boudleaux working together on a song at their house in Gatlinburg in the mid-1980s*

## HARLAN HOWARD ON THE BRYANTS:

"**WHEN I CAME** to town in 1960, they were already going great with the Everly Brothers, Jimmy Dickens, and a bunch of wonderful people. I've never known people more talented. Not only that, they were smarter than the rest of us about the publishing business, about how to conduct their songwriting business. A lot of writers do that nowadays, but us other guys were pretty dumb. So I've always not only admired their ability, I've admired their intelligence."

and roll. Boudleaux, the classically trained violinist turned country/western-swing/jazz fiddler, knew the tropes of rural culture that were still important ingredients of popular music in the late 1940s and 1950s. Felice, steeped in Italian folk tales and folk music as well as American poetry and early twentieth-century movies, knew every classic plotline from popular literature. His music was cerebral and aural; her music was emotional and verbal.

Boudleaux's knowledge of music helped make early country music somewhat more intricate than the three-chords-only songs that had prevailed when he first came to Nashville. And his love of harmony helped the Everlys to display their talents in memorable, heartbreaking duets that grabbed the attention of the world and influenced, in turn, the Beatles, the Beach Boys, the Mamas and the Papas, the Byrds, Simon and Garfunkel, and others.

"ONE OF MY all-time favorite musicians, as well as an idol, was a fellow I used to hear on my two-tube radio, Boudleaux Bryant. When I was a kid I thought his name was Boodle O'Bryant because I had never heard a French word before. I remembered him from when he was on WSB in Atlanta. He did a lot of work with a great country artist, Hank Penny. Boudleaux played classical violin so well that there was a time when he almost made me switch back to fiddle.

"One of the first things I did when I started to get a name for myself and built up a little more confidence was to call Boudleaux. I knew he was living in Nashville at the time, and I also knew he was a great songwriter. He had written hits for Jimmy Dickens and Carl Smith.

"As Boudleaux and I became friends, he used to help me write. We did some jingles for a flour company and it wasn't long before I was hanging out with him a lot. He taught me a lot about classical music because he knew almost every classical piece that had been written. He would teach me the melody, and I would make up my own arrangements.

"When the Carters and I went to New York for a personal appearance, I spent a lot of time in my hotel room. I was lonely, and I wrote the lonesomest melody I could think of. There was a pop song I liked called 'What's New?' so I stole a line from it and titled my song 'How's the World Treating You?' That's how most people get titles—from other songs or from sayings that have stuck with them. I still hear titles and write them down, you know, things I like that people say. When I got back to Nashville, I went right over to Boudleaux's and played the melody for him. 'I like it. You got a name for it?' he asked. 'How's the World Treating You?' I said. He started writing and in a couple of hours he came up with some of the most beautiful lyrics I have ever heard. We both realized it was a good song, so we gave it to Eddy Arnold, who made a hit out of it.

"Another time I was playing an old blues tune for Boudleaux that Jethro [of Homer and Jethro] had taught me, and Boudleaux turned it into 'Midnight.' Red Foley made a great hit out of it.

"Together, we wrote 'Country Gentleman,' which certainly helped my career. It was the first hit record I ever had."

*Felice and Boudleaux, still in love in the mid-1980s*

Nobody knows just how many songs the Bryants wrote, but Dane and Del estimate that their parents finished several thousand compositions and that more than nine hundred have been turned into records. Those songs have sold more than half a *billion* records worldwide. And there'll be more hits from House of Bryant because artists continue to record Bryant songs. In recent years, Norah Jones recorded "Sleepless Nights"; Barry Manilow recorded "All I Have to Do Is Dream"; Rod Stewart recorded "Love Hurts"; Carly Simon recorded "Devoted to You" and "All I Have to Do Is Dream"; and Patti Loveless and Vince Gill recorded "Sleepless Nights."

Boudleaux and Felice were two definite individuals with pronounced personalities and opinions. Together, they

## PAUL MCCARTNEY ON THE BRYANTS:

"I LOVED 'Raining in My Heart,' but only sometime after its release did I learn that Felice and Boudleaux Bryant had written it. I realized then that I had actually been a longtime lover of their compositions without knowing it. They were also good friends of Linda's and mine and we always thought of them as warm and caring people."

were two halves of a whole, neither at all diminished by being one of a pair but, rather, enhanced by the partnership. That communion permeated their lives for forty-two years, giving them the tenacity and strength to endure, on their own terms and uncompromised. In a business where the opinions and even the whims of the public, of recording artists, and of the members of record company hierarchies can determine whether a songwriter makes a living or just doesn't make it, surviving uncompromised is not easy.

# "RAINING IN MY HEART"

**W**hen Boudleaux died in 1987, the music world lost one of its pioneers. Felice received condolence cards and letters from all over the U.S. and England. Many were from people who had not known the Bryants but were fans. Almost all of these used some form of the phrase "thank you for the music." Many of them thanked Felice for the joy the Bryants' music had brought to their youth. The personal friends who wrote to console her realized the magnitude of her—and their—loss. Theodora Zavin, an old friend and a BMI vice president, wrote that when she heard of Boudleaux's passing, she couldn't help thinking of his death as "the fall of a great tree."

Felice couldn't find the energy to reply to all these personal notes. When Boudleaux died, something

*Boudleaux and Felice with Dane and Del at the 1986 induction dinner for the National Academy of Popular Music's Songwriters Hall of Fame in New York*

*Felice and Boudleaux with Harry Warner, Isaac Hayes, Little Richard, Buddy Bowie and Frances Preston after the 1986 Songwriters Hall of Fame induction dinner*

in Felice died, too—she had lost the love of her life, her mate, her cowriter, her business partner. She said, "Boudleaux had a sense of humor. He was witty, he was clever. Everything you'd want, he had. And I was as brave as anything he ever ran into. With him, I couldn't lose. But it's very hard without him. It's like a power failure that's not repaired." Felice had always been the life of every party, but after Boudleaux's death she pined for him and became reclusive. For a girl brought up among Sicilian Catholic women who donned black when their husbands died and spent the rest of their lives in mourning, it was a predictable response. She summed up her feelings in an unsent, handwritten letter to fellow national Songwriters Hall of Fame member Jimmy Webb shortly after Boudleaux's death. She wrote, "I've tried many times to answer your very tender letter regarding my Boudleaux, but I can't seem to put my feelings into words at this time. I'm still in a strange place after the loss of my friend, and I'm trying hard to come out of the fog that used to be cloud nine. Thank you for your good wishes and blessings."

After Boudleaux's death, Felice continued to live in the beautiful house in Gatlinburg, Tennessee where she and Boudleaux had lived, and she seldom left Gatlinburg for any reason. She ran House of Bryant Publications, the music publishing company that had been the family enterprise since 1967, and managed the Rocky Top Village Inn, the Gatlinburg motel that Boudleaux had bought to run as a hobby. She also gave away a lot of money, to refugees, to religious groups, and to children's charities—the Ronald McDonald House in Knoxville got both her classic bottle-green Mercedes sedan and Boudleaux's vintage Rolls-Royce Silver Cloud. She abandoned writing. Several established songwriters made themselves available to write with her in the years after Boudleaux's death and her sons prevailed upon her to work for a few days with some of them, but her heart wasn't in it. In the end, she gave up the effort to re-create the partnership she had had with her husband. Typically, she summed up her feelings in a humorous but telling quip: "I don't want to write anymore," she said. "I ran that race, and I won it."

At one point during the late 1990s however, a friend showed Felice some of the many websites and articles about the Bryants available on the Internet, with which

Felice was unfamiliar. She viewed a few of them, laughed over quotations from interviews she had forgotten, and came away with a renewed sense of the impact she and Boudleaux had made on popular music. She said, "We made a big noise, didn't we?"

The Bryants' sons, Dane and Del, have remained involved in the music business. After working for some years as a studio owner and music publisher, Dane became a commercial real estate agent, selling and leasing buildings up and down Nashville's Music Row. After working for Broadcast Music, Inc. for most of his adult life, Del became president and CEO of BMI in 2004. The Bryant boys have given their parents five grandchildren—a chef, a schoolteacher, a nurse, a health-industry executive, and a little boy named Thaddeus who was fascinated with violins even before he could read. Boudleaux and Felice also have six great-grandchildren, two boys and four girls.

## "THEME FROM A DREAM"

**T**he Bryants' peers in the music industry valued and recognized their contributions to popular music. Over the many years of their affiliation with BMI, the airplay for their songs has earned them a total of fifty-nine Pop, Country, and R&B awards. In tribute to Boudleaux's birth in Shellman, Georgia, and to their early efforts at songwriting there, both Boudleaux and Felice were made members of the Georgia Music Hall of Fame, Boudleaux in 1982 and Felice in 2006. They were named members of the Rockabilly Hall of Fame because of their contribution to the music of the rockabilly era (1955–1960, roughly). They were inducted into the Nashville Songwriters Hall of Fame in 1972 and, in 1986, into the National Academy of Popular Music's Songwriters Hall of Fame, at a glitzy dinner at the Plaza Hotel in New York, along with Chuck Berry,

*Felice with her three granddaughters, Felice, Dana, and Heather*

*Thaddeus Bryant, Boudleaux and Felice's youngest grandchild*

*Felice onstage accepting for herself and Boudleaux, after their induction into the Country Music Hall of Fame in 1991*

Buddy Holly (a posthumous inductee), Jimmy Webb, and Marvin Hamlisch. In 2006 they, along with Roy Orbison, Reba McEntire, Ronnie Milsap, Fisk University's Jubilee Singers, and Nashville Symphony conductor Kenneth Schermerhorn, were honored with stars in the first induction ceremony for Nashville's Walk of Fame, in a spot Boudleaux would have relished—at the beginning of Nashville's Music Mile in front of the Country Music Hall of Fame and just across the street from Nashville's magnificent new Schermerhorn Symphony Hall.

Perhaps the most moving of these honors came in 1991, when the Bryants were inducted into the Country Music Hall of Fame. It was an emotional night for Felice, mostly because she missed her songwriting partner and knew how much the honor would have meant to him. She was also nervous. She knew that if she and Boudleaux were

announced as new inductees, she would have to make an
acceptance speech, in the middle of the Opry House stage,
on live national television. But, as she had done her whole
life, she conquered her fear when the time came. Her sons
walked her up the short set of stairs to the stage and returned
to their seats, leaving their little mom standing alone in her
blue dress in front of hundreds of her peers watching her
live and millions of country music fans watching her on
TV. She said, "My secretary wrote a speech for me, Dane
wrote a speech for me, and Del wrote a speech for me, but
I'm speechless. If Boudleaux were here, he would thank
everybody. Thank you." Then, in a quip that was vintage
Felice, she looked toward the front rows of the audience,
where the first President Bush and his wife were sitting. She
addressed Barbara Bush, "And, Barbara, I'm so glad you
brought Georgie with you." The audience exploded with
laughter and applause as Felice appealed in an aside to
another Barbara, Barbara Mandrell, who was standing
onstage behind her, "Barbara, get me out of here!"
Barbara Mandrell complied and escorted the nervous new Hall of Fame inductee backstage. It was
the last time Felice ever appeared before a large
audience. Felice Bryant died in Gatlinburg in
2003; she was 77. Like Boudleaux,
she received that uncommon
posthumous honor, an obitu-
ary in the *New York Times*.

The Bryants brought
joy to millions. And although

we miss them, we still have their songs. Hundreds of pop and country artists have recorded more than nine hundred of their compositions, and more than half a billion records of their tunes have been sold. They were capable of creating haunting country ballads, poignant teenage anthems, and witty up-tempo tunes with lyrics and melodies that, for several decades, captivated everyone in the world who owned a turntable or turned on a radio. Their songs colored the greater part of the twentieth century and are likely to remain mainstays of popular culture for most of the current century. In fact, because the themes of popular music haven't changed much since the Renaissance, it's likely that the great-grandchildren of some of the people who first loved the Bryants' songs will listen to them and sing them and feel that, somehow, those songs were written about *their* romances, *their* broken hearts, and *their* lives.

*Felice and Boudleaux,
gone but not
forgotten*

# THE BRYANT HIT PARADE

A few of the songs written by Boudleaux and Felice Bryant and some of the artists who recorded them (listed in alphabetical order under each song):

The Everly Brothers

Don Gibson and Dottie West

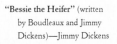

Glen Campbell and Bobbie Gentry

"A Change of Heart"—the Everly Brothers, Kitty Wells

"A Screwball's Love Song" (written by Boudleaux)—Homer and Jethro

"All I Have to Do Is Dream" (written by Boudleaux)—Jeff Bridges and Juice Newton, Richard Chamberlain, the Everly Brothers, Bobbie Gentry and Glen Campbell, Andy Gibb and Victoria Principal, George Harrison, Jan and Dean, Gary Lewis and the Playboys, Barry Manilow, Nancy Montgomery, Nitty Gritty Dirt Band, the Nylons, the Osborne Brothers, R.E.M., Carly Simon, Roger Whittaker

"Always It's You"—the Everly Brothers

"Back Up, Buddy" (written by Boudleaux)—Carl Smith

"Baltimore"—Sonny James

"Before the Ring on Your Finger Turns Green"—Dottie West

"Bessie the Heifer" (written by Boudleaux and Jimmy Dickens)—Jimmy Dickens

Carly Simon

Sonny James

Nitty Gritty Dirt Band

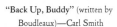

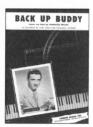

Carl Smith

Trini Lopez

Roy Orbison

Ray Charles

Gary Lewis and the Playboys

Roy Clark

Jimmy Dickens

Homer and Jethro
and June Carter

"Bird Dog" (written by Boudleaux)—the Bellamy Brothers, the Everly Brothers, Carl Perkins

"Blue Boy" (written by Boudleaux)—Charley Pride, Jim Reeves

"Bye, Bye, Love"—Bobby Bare, Ray Charles, Floyd Cramer, Rita Coolidge, Lacy J. Dalton and Eddie Rabbitt, the Everly Brothers, Connie Francis, George Harrison, the Montovani Orchestra, Roy Orbison, Donnie Osmond, Webb Pierce, the Platters, Del Reeves, the Righteous Brothers, Jimmie Rodgers, Simon and Garfunkel, Trini Lopez, Conway Twitty and Loretta Lynn

"Chaplin in New Shoes" (written by Boudleaux)—Chet Atkins, Al Hirt, Boots Randolph

"Christmas Can't Be Far Away" (written by Boudleaux)—Eddy Arnold, Burl Ives

"Come Live with Me"—Ray Charles, Roy Clark

"Copy Cat"—Cowboy and Kathy Copas

"Country Boy"—Jimmy Dickens, Ricky Skaggs

"Country Gentleman" (written by Boudleaux and Chet Atkins)—Chet Atkins, Arthur Fiedler and the Boston Pops, the Nashville Brass

"Country Girl"—Homer and Jethro with June Carter

*Sue Thompson*

*Cowboy and Kathy Copas*

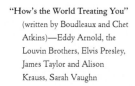

*Frankie Laine*

"**Devoted to You**" (written by Boudleaux)—the Beach Boys, the Everly Brothers, Brian Hyland, Linda Ronstadt, Carly Simon and James Taylor

"**Fall Away**"—Eddie Albert, Bill Anderson, Archie Campbell, Tex Ritter

"**Frangipani**"—Burl Ives

"**Have a Good Time**"—Tony Bennett, Ruth Brown, Billy Eckstine, Peggy March, Jimmy Rogers, Hank Thompson, Sue Thompson, Sarah Vaughn

"**Hawk-Eye**" (written by Boudleaux)—Frankie Laine, Bobby Lord

"**Hey, Joe**" (written by Boudleaux)—Moe Bandy and Joe Stampley, Cab Calloway, Frank Ifield, Frankie Laine, Carl Smith, the Statler Brothers, Kitty Wells

"**How's the World Treating You**" (written by Boudleaux and Chet Atkins)—Eddy Arnold, the Louvin Brothers, Elvis Presley, James Taylor and Alison Krauss, Sarah Vaughn

"**I Can Hear Kentucky Calling Me**"—Chet Atkins, the Osborne Brothers, Billie Jo Spears, Steve Wariner, Roger Whittaker

"**I'd Rather Stay Home**"— Kitty Wells

"**I Love to Dance with Annie**"— Ernest Ashworth

*Tony Bennett*

*Tex Ritter*

*Bobby Lord*

*Elvis Presley*

*Eddy Arnold*

*The Oak Ridge Boys*

*Red Foley*

*Bob Moore*

**"I'm Little but I'm Loud"** (written by Boudleaux and Jimmy Dickens)—Jimmy Dickens, Martina McBride

**"I'm Not Afraid"** (written by Felice)—George Morgan, Ricky Nelson

**"It's a Lovely, Lovely World"** (written by Boudleaux)—Gail Davies, Carl Smith

**"I've Been Thinking"** (written by Boudleaux)—Eddy Arnold, Rusty Draper, the Four Lads

**"(I've Got) a Hole in My Pocket"**—Jimmy Dickens, Ricky Van Shelton

**"Jackass Blues"** (written by Boudleaux)—Elton Britt

**"Just Wait Till I Get You Alone"**—Carl Smith

**"Let's Think About Living"** (written by Boudleaux)—Red Foley, Trini Lopez, Bob Luman, Del Reeves, Soupy Sales

**"Like Strangers"** (written by Boudleaux)—Gail Davies, the Everly Brothers, Emmylou Harris, Cliff Richard

**"Love Hurts"** (written by Boudleaux)—Jim Capaldi, Cher, the Everly Brothers, Emmylou Harris and Gram Parsons, Joan Jett, Norah Jones, Don McLean, Garry Morrison, Nazareth, Roy Orbison, Linda Ronstadt, Jennifer Warnes, Jimmy Webb, Yndio

*Kitty Wells*

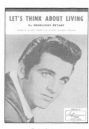

*Ricky Nelson*

*Bob Luman*

*Don McLean*

*The Osborne Brothers*

*Emmylou Harris*

*Buddy Holly*

*Chet Atkins*

"Midnight" (written by Boudleaux and Chet Atkins)—Ray Charles, Red Foley

"Mexico" (written by Boudleaux)—Herb Alpert and the Tijuana Brass, Bob Moore, the Ventures

"Muddy Bottom"—the Osborne Brothers

"My Last Date" (written by Boudleaux, Floyd Cramer, and Skeeter Davis)—Skeeter Davis

"Our Honeymoon"—Carl Smith

"Out Behind the Barn" (written by Boudleaux)—Jimmy Dickens

"Pay Day"—Porter Wagoner

"Penny Arcade"—Eddy Arnold, Cyrkle, Cristy Lane,

"Poor Jenny"—the Everly Brothers

"Problems"—Ray Charles, the Everly Brothers

"Raining in My Heart"—Connie Francis, Buddy Holly, Kitty Kallen, Dean Martin, Don McLean, Anne Murray, Johnny Nash, Ray Price, Leo Sayer, Jo-El Sonnier, Ringo Starr, Johnny Tillotson, Bobby Vee, Bobby Vinton

"The Richest Man (in the World)" (written by Boudleaux)—Eddy Arnold

*Nazareth*

*George Jones*

*Leo Sayer*

*Jim Reeves*

Gail Davies

The Judds

Hank Williams

TAKE A MESSAGE TO MARY

Bob Dylan

"Rocky Top"— Chet Atkins,
Bill Anderson, Lynn Anderson,
Glen Campbell, the Osborne
Brothers, Buck Owens, Dolly
Parton, Phish, Boots Randolph,
Dinah Shore, Conway Twitty,
Porter Wagoner

"Salty Boogie"—Jimmy Dickens

"She Wears My Ring"—Eddy
Arnold, Solomon King,
Elvis Presley, Ray Price, Roy
Orbison, the Wanderers

"Sleepless Nights"—Jerry Byrd,
Elvis Costello, the Everly
Brothers, Norah Jones, the
Judds, Emmylou Harris and
Gram Parsons, Jimmie Rodgers

"So How Come (No One Loves
Me)"—the Beatles, the Everly
Brothers

"Somebody's Stolen My
Honey" (written by
Boudleaux)—Ernest Tubb

"Sugar Beet" (written by
Boudleaux)—Moon Mullican

"Sweet Deceiver"—Cristy Lane

"Take a Message to Mary"—
Chet Atkins, Don Cherry, Bob
Dylan, the Everly Brothers

"Take Me as I Am (or Let
Me Go)" (written by
Boudleaux)—Bobby Bare,
Roy Clark, Jimmy Dickens,
Bob Dylan, George Jones, the
Osborne Brothers, Ray Price,
Mack White

Ernest Tubb

Lynn Anderson

Moon Mullican

Tony Orlando

*Johnny and Jack*

*The Everly Brothers*

*Charley Pride*

"**Tennessee Hound Dog**" (written by Boudleaux)— the Osborne Brothers

"**Theme From a Dream**" (written by Boudleaux)—Chet Atkins, Floyd Cramer, Al Hirt

"**Time**" (written by Boudleaux)— Sarah Vaughan

"**Time's A Wastin'**" (written by Boudleaux)—Carl Smith and June Carter

"**Wake Up, Little Susie**"— Joe Cocker, Billy "Crash" Craddock, the Everly Brothers, the Flying Burrito Brothers, the Grateful Dead, Loggins and Messina, Ricky Nelson, Donnie Osmond, Billy Joe Royal, Simon and Garfunkel

"**We Could**" (written by Felice)— Roy Clark, Jimmy Dickens, Stonewall Jackson, George Jones and Tammy Wynette, the Louvin Brothers, Al Martino, George Morgan, the Osborne Brothers, Charley Pride, John Prine, Jim Reeves, Jean Sheppard and Ray Pillow, Billie Jo Spears and Carey Duncan, Kitty Wells

"**Where Did the Sunshine Go**"—Jimmy Dickens, George Jones, the Osborne Brothers, Porter Wagoner

"**Willie Can**"—Alma Cogan, Mitch Miller

"**You Weren't Ashamed to Kiss Me Last Night**"—Ray Price

*Simon and Garfunkel*

*Donnie Osmond*

*Porter Wagoner*

# ACKNOWLEDGMENTS

ALL I HAVE TO DO IS DREAM:
THE BOUDLEAUX AND FELICE
BRYANT STORY

WRITER: Lee Wilson

PHOTO RESEARCHER AND EDITOR: Lee Wilson

BOOK DESIGN: Bruce Gore | Gore Studio, Inc.,
Brentwood, Tennessee

PHOTOS: photos on pages 79, 105, 116 (bottom), 117, 119 (top), 127, and 128, BMI;
photos on page 38, Wayne Daniel; photo on
page 42, Georgia Music Hall of Fame: Lisa
Love; photos on pages 49, 53, Metropolitan
Nashville Archives; photo on page 119 (bottom),
*The Tennessean*; photo on page 118 (bottom),
University of Tennessee Pride of the Southland
Band; photo on page 20, Wisconsin Historical
Society; all other photos courtesy of Dane and
Del Bryant and House of Bryant Publications

ACKNOWLEDGMENTS
Thanks: Chet Atkins; Eddy Arnold; Clare
Bratten; "The Beehive," the Official Everly
Brothers Fan Club: John Hosum; BMI
Nashville: Olivia Gordon; BMI New York:
Dave Sanjek; Bobby Bare; City of Moultrie;
Kitty Cole; the Country Music Hall of Fame
and Museum: John Rumble, Tim Davis, Alan
Stoker, Michael Gray; Wayne Daniel; Jimmy
Dickens; Greg Eckler; Ralph Emery; Don
Everly; Phil Everly; Fred Foster; Gaylord
Entertainment Company TV Archives: Sandy
Liles; Georgia Music Hall of Fame: Lisa Love;
Jeri Hasty; House of Bryant Publications:
Susan Jenkins; Fred Koller; Bucky Lindsey; the
Metropolitan Government Archives of Nashville
and Davidson County; the Museum of Colquitt
County History; Danise Nabarro; The Nashville
Room of the Nashville Public Library; Opry
Museum: Brenda Colladay; Orbison Records:
Barbara Orbison, Cass Paley; Tom Roland; Rick
Sanjek; Tennessee Ernie Ford Enterprises; The
Tennessee State Library and Archives; Greg
Tornquist; the University of Tennessee Pride of
the Southland Band: Dorothy Bryson; Porter
Wagoner; the Wisconsin Historical Society: Dee
Grimsrud; and Johnny Wright and Kitty Wells
for their contributions to the ALL I HAVE TO
DO IS DREAM project.

Boudleaux and Felice Bryant were proud to be
affiliate writers of Broadcast Music, Inc.

FOR PERMISSION TO USE ANY
HOUSE OF BRYANT SONG, PLEASE CONTACT:
House of Bryant Publications
P.O. Box 570, Gatlinburg, Tennessee 37738
(865) 436-6351
or write HOBPublications@aol.com.

Lightning Source UK Ltd.
Milton Keynes UK
UKRC011805040119
334996UK00001B/34